CHAPTER TWO: SKILLS AND KNOWLEDGE
Democracy in Scotland

Scottish Parliament Committees

The Work of an MSP

Voting and the Additional Member System

The Media and the 2011 Scottish Elections

Local councils in Scotland

Participation in Trade Unions in Scotland and the UK

ACKNOWLEDGEMENTS

DEMOCRACY IN SCOTLAND AND THE UNITED KINGDOM by John McTaggart & Suzanna Kerr

ISBN 978-0-9555750-2-0. First published March 2013. Published by 241 Media Ltd for Modernity Scotland.

All copyright reserved 241 Media Ltd 2013. No reproduction allowed without express written permission from publishers.

Bulk photocopying prohibited. Enquires email info@241media.co.uk

Thanks to the team at 241 Media , especially Suzanne Waters for design and typesetting and Suzanna Kerr for editing.

Thanks to the following for photograph permissions; BBC, Scottish Government.

Thanks to Mark Mackarel, Helen Raw, Hillsborough Justice Group, SPOKES, Cllr Dave Dempsey and Cllr Lesley Laird, Jo Swinson MP, Humza Yousaf MSP.

Published and Designed by 241 Media Ltd , 10 Somerset Place, Glasgow G3 7JT on behalf of Modernityscotland. 3 Hawkcraig Road, Aberdour KY3 0UP.

www.modernityscotland.co.uk

03

CHAPTER THREE: SKILLS AND KNOWLEDGE

Democracy in the UK

The Work of an MP

Reform of the House of Lords

Voting and the First Past the Post Voting System

The Media and the General Election 2010

Pressure groups in Scotland and the UK

CHAPTER FOUR: APPLYING THE SKILLS AND KNOWLEDGE

Assessment

Modern Studies Assignment Topics or Issues

Using Sources of Information

National 4 Modern Studies Assessment

National 5 Modern Studies Assessment

04

05

Introd

WELCOME TO DEMOCRACY IN SCOTLAND AND THE UNITED KINGDOM.

In this book we look at the democratic institutions and processes in Scotland and within the UK.

The issue of Scotland's place within the United Kingdom is likely to be the subject of debate for some time. The re-establishment of the Scottish Parliament in 1999 did not end speculation about Scotland's constitutional future. If anything, it has raised the issue of more decision-making power to be devolved to Scotland, including, ultimately, Scottish independence.

One of the aims of Modern Studies and Curriculum for Excellence as a whole is that you will become an informed and engaged citizen; aware and confident about your rights and responsibilities in your local community, Scotland and the UK. This book aims to provide you with the knowledge which will assist you in this aspiration, as well as assist you with your Modern Studies qualification at National 4 or National 5.

In the National 4/5 Democracy in Scotland and the United Kingdom Unit you will study either Democracy in Scotland or Democracy in the United Kingdom. You will not study both. However, whatever option you study, it is important for you to understand the ideas of democracy within the UK and the main institutions which impact upon democracy at both a Scottish and a UK level. This is why all learners should read Chapter One and possibly take part in its Learning Activities. After that you will read either Chapter Two or Chapter Three (although you are very welcome to read both!) Chapter Four, with its emphasis on the Assignment (National

uction

4 and 5) and the Question Paper (National 5 only), is relevant for all who are taking this Unit.

The Democracy in Scotland and the United Kingdom Unit is one Unit of National 4/5 Modern Studies. There are strong links between what you learn in Democracy in Scotland and the United Kingdom and in the other two units of the Modern Studies course; Social Issues in the United Kingdom and International Issues. For example, an awareness of the devolved powers the Scottish Parliament has will result in a better understanding of how successful the Scottish Government can be in tackling poverty. Likewise, an understanding of how another country tackles crime will result in a richer understanding of Scottish Government approaches to crime.

MODERN STUDIES IS FOR LIFE

"Modern Studies is an exciting subject which provides an excellent overview of the main political institutions and processes in the UK. It is useful for a wide variety of careers and many of our students enjoyed Modern Studies at school."

Mark Mackarel, Lecturer in International Criminal Law, University of Dundee

This book contains lots of facts, evidence and what can be termed 'Skills and Knowledge'.

The skills Modern Studies develops are:

- **Using sources of information to detect and explain exaggeration and selectivity in the use of facts**

- **Using sources of information to justify decisions**

- **Using sources of information to draw and support valid conclusions**

We exaggerate when we say something is bigger, better, smaller or worse than it really is. We can prove a person is exaggerating when we compare what they are saying with the evidence. Sometimes a politician, pressure group or media organisation may deliberately make exaggerated statements in order to persuade people towards a particular point of view.

Being selective in the use of facts is slightly different. This is when a person only highlights particular information which suits their point of view, ignoring other evidence which may not suit the point they are trying to make. Politicians and others are often selective in the use of facts as they highlight evidence which supports what they are trying to say. Sometimes they employ specially trained media people known as "spin doctors" to help them "spin" the information to the public.

We use sources of information to justify choices we make. Often in Modern Studies there is no one perfect decision. But some decisions are better than others. When you can support what you recommend with evidence then that is a decision you can justify. Also, being able to evaluate the usefulness of a source is a skill too. Some sources of information are more reliable than others. Some may be biased, that is, they come from a person or organisation with a particular point to prove. Other information may be more independent. It is up to us to use our judgement on how much we trust the information which we are provided with.

A valid conclusion is one which a reasonable person might make after looking at different points of view and weighing up the evidence. It says something about trends over time; whether things have improved, got worse, whether a policy has been successful or not. It may not be perfect, indeed in social and political issues there rarely is a perfect solution everyone will agree with. But some conclusions and decisions are better than others. Those which can be supported by evidence and reason are better than those which cannot be supported by evidence and reason.

So these are the skills you will be assessed in throughout your Modern Studies course. They are also highly valuable for your life outside of school and later on in the world of education and work. I'm sure you can think of many occasions when someone exaggerates or is selective in their use of facts. Making informed choices, based on evidence is a lifelong skill, valued in a wide range of occupations. You can achieve success at either National 4 or National 5 depending on how well you can demonstrate your acquisition of these Modern Studies skills.

Modern Studies is also about developing a knowledge and understanding of contemporary society. In this book we have learning activities that allow you to demonstrate your knowledge and understanding of Democracy in Scotland and the United Kingdom. Depending on how well you can demonstrate your knowledge and understanding of either Democracy in Scotland or Democracy in the United Kingdom, you can achieve at either National 4 or National 5.

Modern Studies, like the other social studies qualifications, also provides the opportunity for you to apply your skills and knowledge in an area of your choice. So in both National 4 and National 5 — through the Modern Studies Assignment — you will be asked to research and use information collected from a range of sources. This is your opportunity to select an issue you are particularly interested in. It can be an issue from any of the three units from the Modern Studies Course. At National 4, there are a wide variety of ways you can present this information. In this book, we shall offer some suggestions on how you can carry out the Modern Studies Assignment on an issue within Democracy in Scotland and the United Kingdom. You will find this information on pages 117–125. Please note that these are only suggestions — they are not compulsory and whatever you choose to study and how you present it should be discussed with your teacher.

INTERNAL ASSESSMENT NATIONAL 4 AND NATIONAL 5

Throughout both the Democracy in Scotland and Democracy in the United Kingdom options in the book there are a number of Learning Activities. These are suggested ways in which you can reinforce knowledge and develop Modern Studies skills. They are not split into National 4 or National 5 activities as whether you are presented at National 4 or National 5 is something you need to agree with your teacher.

The Modern Studies skills at National 5 are more challenging than the skills at National 4. Likewise, the National 5, the main difference between knowledge at National 5 and National 4 is the quality of detail and exemplification provided. So, Learning Activities stress the importance of "detail" in your response wherever possible.

Chapter Four is the only chapter which has different content for National 4 and National 5 learners. Here, because of the different assessment arrangements we have advice for National 4 and National 5 but also illustrative examples of the kind of external assessments National 5 learners may experience.

In order to achieve the Modern Studies course award at either National 4 or National 5 you must pass the internal assessments from the three units of the course:

- **Democracy in Scotland and the UK**

- **Social Issues in the United Kingdom**

- **International Issues**

At National 4, you must also pass the Modern Studies Assignment. Like the assessments in the other three units, the National 4 Modern Studies Assignment is internally assessed by your teacher. Awards in National 4 Modern Studies are on a pass or fail basis.

EXTERNAL ASSESSMENT (NATIONAL 5)

At National 5 you need to pass the internal assessments (see above) and the Modern Studies Course Assessment, which is externally assessed by SQA.

The Course Assessment is composed of:

- **The National 5 Modern Studies Question Paper**
- **The National 5 Modern Studies Assignment**

Awards in National 5 Modern Studies are graded A, B, C and D.

We hope you enjoy this book and your Modern Studies course!

Chapter One:
Skills and Knowledge

Democracy in Scotland and the United Kingdom

DEMOCRACY

Democracy is a form of government in which all citizens have a say in the decisions that affect their lives. Democracy allows citizens to participate equally—either directly or through elected representatives—in the proposal and creation of laws.

The term democracy originates from the Greek word dēmokratía "rule of the people". Countries which have a democratic form of government normally have regular elections. People are free to vote for whoever they choose, or not to vote at all. People are free to form their political parties or groups. They are free to criticize the Government and express their point of view at meetings, in print or online.

Not all democracies are the same. The USA, for example is a democracy. But it is a Republic, where there is no monarch and the head of state, the President, is elected directly by the people.

The UK is a constitutional monarchy where the monarch is the head of state. The monarch approves laws which are made by the UK Parliament, which has two houses; the House of Commons and the House of Lords.

Democracy has developed in the UK and is still developing.

Since 1999, power within the UK has moved away from Westminster towards the nations which make up the UK. This process is called devolution. The people of Northern Ireland, Scotland and Wales have been given their own parliaments, giving them more say in what happens in their countries.

12

UK Prime Ministers no longer have the right to call a General Election at a time of their own choosing. In 2011 Parliament passed the historic Fixed-term Parliaments Bill which means that General Elections will take place every five years.

The UK has not always been a democracy. Parliament had to fight to win power from the monarchy. And not everyone has always had the right to vote. For example, in the past, only men had the right to vote. However, since 1928 all adults in the UK have had the right to vote. In 1969 the age a person could vote was reduced to 18.

RIGHTS AND RESPONSIBILITIES

Countries which are Republics tend to have written constitutions, which explain the role of each part of Government and the rights citizens within that country have.

The UK does not have a written constitution. Instead, the UK is governed by a set of unwritten ways of working which have developed over the centuries.

Since World War Two international bodies such as the United Nations and the European Union have devised a series of conventions which spell out the rights all people should be entitled to.

In 1948 the United Nations adopted the Universal Declaration of Human Rights (UDHR). Its thirty articles set out, for the first time, the rights and freedoms all human beings should have.

Since October 2000, the UK Human Rights Act (HRA) has made rights from the European Convention on Human Rights enforceable in UK courts.

These rights include:

- **Right to life**

- **Freedom from torture and inhuman or degrading treatment**

- **Right to liberty and security**

- **Freedom from slavery and forced labour**

- **Right to a fair trial**

- **No punishment without law**

- **Respect for your private and family life, home and correspondence**

- **Freedom of thought, belief and religion**

- **Freedom of expression**

- **Freedom of assembly and association**

- **Right to marry and start a family**

- **Protection from discrimination in respect of these rights and freedoms**

  - **Right to peaceful enjoyment of your property**

- **Right to education**

LEARNING ACTIVITY: HUMAN RIGHTS IN SCHOOL SURVEY

In this activity you can evaluate how well your school promotes the human rights all of us are supposed to have.

Carry out a survey of learners in your class on human rights within your school. Ask people to rate each answer on a scale of 1–5, with 5 being the best, on how well the following human rights are respected.

1. I am not discriminated against because of my race, sex, family background, disability or religion.
    (UDHR articles 2 and 16)

2. My school is a place where I am safe and secure.
    (UDHR articles 3 and 5)

3. All learners receive equal information and encouragement about academic and career opportunities.
    (UDHR articles 2 and 26)

5. Staff in my school oppose any discriminatory actions, materials or words in the school.
    (UDHR articles 2, 3, 7, 28 and 29)

6. I have the opportunity to participate in cultural activities at school and my cultural identity, language and values are respected. *(UDHR articles 19, 27 and 28)*

7. No one in our school is subjected to degrading treatment or punishment.*(UDHR article 5)*

8. Someone accused of wrong–doing is presumed innocent until proved guilty. *(UDHR article 11)*

9. My personal space and possessions are respected.
    (UDHR articles 12 and 17)

10. Learners in my school have the opportunity to participate in democratic decision–making to develop school policies and rules.
    (UDHR articles 20, 21 and 23)

PRESENT YOUR FINDINGS:

Use a balance of bar charts, pie charts and written conclusions. Record and present the date(s) of your survey.

Draw conclusions, detailed if possible, on human rights in your school.

Comment on how valid and/or reliable the evidence is in your survey.

For example, do you think all the answers are honest? Do you think answers would be more honest if the responses were anonymous?

What about the size of your survey? Did you interview enough people to make it meaningful?

While we all have rights, we also have responsibilities. There's always got to be a balance between a right, something we are entitled to and a responsibility, something we owe to other people.

School is the most obvious one. We all have the right to education but we all have the responsibility not to disrupt lessons and prevent others from their right to education.

We have the responsibility to obey the law even if we don't agree with it. In 2006, the Scottish Government introduced the ban on smoking in enclosed public spaces. Those who do not smoke now have the right not to breathe second-hand smoke. Those who do smoke have the responsibility to obey the law and to go outside to smoke. Any bar or restaurant which allows people to smoke indoors runs the risk of losing their license to do business.

We have the responsibility to pay our taxes. Those who are employed have their tax contributions deducted by their employer. But the self-employed have the responsibility to complete a tax return and honestly declare any earned income. Few people like paying taxes. But taxes pay for our hospitals, schools and all the other public services we can't do without.

Many other responsibilities can be moral, rather legal. For example, in how we conduct ourselves in our daily lives. Do we treat people the way we expect to be treated ourselves? Do we care for the feelings of others? Are we tolerant of people who have different beliefs or ways of life than ourselves?

It's not illegal to be a nasty person but people who have self-respect and respect others are usually more popular and successful in life.

PARLIAMENT:
THE HOUSE OF COMMONS

Parliament is responsible for approving new laws (legislation). The government introduces most plans for new laws, or changes to existing laws – but they can originate from an MP, Lord or even a member of the public or private group. Before they can become law, both the House of Commons and House of Lords must debate and vote on the proposals.

At a UK level, there are three parts to the decision making process. Firstly, Members of Parliament (MPs) are elected to the House of Commons. MPs work to make the laws and also check the actions of the Government. Secondly, Peers in the House of Lords check the laws made in the House of Commons. Lastly, the monarch, as head of state, plays a mostly symbolic role in parliamentary procedures.

There are 650 MPs elected to the House of Commons. Each MP represents a local area (called a constituency). An MP is paid £65,738 per year (January 2013). Some MPs are paid more because of the special jobs they hold. For example, the Speaker and the Chairs of Committees receive an extra salary.

Most MPs who are also ministers in the Government are paid an extra ministerial salary. MPs are entitled to a range of expenses which they occur in doing their work. These costs can be due to communicating with constituents, hiring office space and staff or travel and accommodation. In 2010 there was a serious scandal when many MPs were found to be over–claiming expenses.

Members of the Commons (MPs) debate the big political issues of the day and proposals for new laws. It is one of the key places where government ministers, like the Prime Minister and the Chancellor, and the principal figures of the main political parties, work.

The Commons alone is responsible for making decisions on financial Bills, such as proposed new taxes. The Lords can consider these Bills but cannot block or amend them.

SCRUTINY OF THE GOVERNMENT

MPs check the work of the government on behalf of UK citizens through asking government ministers questions during parliamentary sessions. They can also join a variety of select committees which make sure government ministers are doing their job properly.

MPs question government ministers and expect to be answered orally or in writing. Ministers from each government department attend the Commons on a rota basis to answer oral questions. The Prime Minister answers questions every Wednesday.

DEBATES AND VOTES

Debates in the Commons can sometimes be noisy and badly behaved! MPs are constantly trying to 'catch the eye' of The Speaker to be allowed to speak. At other times, when a Bill is less controversial, the Commons can be very quiet. Votes are often taken to see whether a majority of Members either support or reject any discussed laws or proposals. It is the job of Government 'whips' to ensure that MPs from the governing party support the Government in their vote. On these occasions MPs can sometimes have a conflict between the wishes of their party and the wishes of their constituents.

COMMITTEES

The Commons has groups of MPs who look at specific policy issues or legislation in detail. The government issues responses to most committee reports.

PARLIAMENT: THE HOUSE OF LORDS

The House of Lords has around 760 members (January 2013), referred to as 'peers'. Most peers have been appointed by the Prime Minister, sometimes in recognition of their expertise in a particular area. Some are Church of England bishops. Others are 'hereditary' peers, that is, they inherited their membership of the Lords from their father. The House

of Lords is the second biggest legislature in the world after China's National People's Congress.

Peers can claim £300 or a lower rate of £150 per day tax free. The pressure group Unlock Democracy found that in 2011, a combined total of 75 peers claimed over £46,000 despite failing to vote on any parliamentary business. One peer, the Earl of Rosslyn, allegedly claimed over £15,000 despite not voting at all or sitting on any parliamentary committees.

The House of Lords is the second chamber of the UK Parliament. It complements the work of the House of Commons. It makes laws, holds government to account and investigates policy issues.

The main role of the House of Lords is to debate and revise major legislation, but peers also have the freedom and time to discuss other national issues as they arise. Peers in the Lords have greater flexibility to examine an issue for longer than is typical in the Commons. Peers in the House of Lords aren't under the same pressure to vote with their party as MPs in the Commons are. Because of these factors, supporters of the Lords argue that peers make a vital contribution to the quality of legislation.

THE EUROPEAN UNION

The UK is one of 27 member states of the European Union and is subject to European Union (EU) legislation.

The EU has the authority to apply legislation in the UK but actually putting it into action may require Parliament to pass new or amended legislation. There is a possibility of a referendum on the UK's continued membership of the EU at some point in the future.

THE PRIME MINISTER AND THE FIRST MINISTER

Unlike in the USA where there are direct elections for the head of state, UK voters do not vote directly for the UK Prime Minister (who also, of course, is not head of state). Instead, the Prime Minister is the leader of the political party which has won the most seats in a General Election.

Like other institutions in British politics, the role of the Prime Minister has evolved over time. As Parliament replaced the monarchy as the UK's decision making body, the monarch required a head of government who could command a majority in Parliament.

The modern Prime Minister is head of The Cabinet and his/her role is best understood as 'first among equals'. The Prime Minister selects the most capable MPs to be Government Ministers. The Prime Minister of the United Kingdom of Great Britain and Northern Ireland is the head of Her Majesty's Government in the United Kingdom.

The Prime Minister and Cabinet are collectively accountable for their policies and actions to the monarch and to Parliament. The Prime Minister must appear before Parliament each week and answer questions from MPs at Prime Minister's Question Time. Prime Minister's Question Time is mostly about performing for the television cameras. Government policy is highly unlikely to be changed by an opposition question. But a Prime Minister who is confident and assured at Prime Minister's Question Time can impress the voters. By doing so, he/she will improve their MPs' morale. The opposite is also the case! So, Prime Minister's Question Time can be quite important.

Because of the nature of the modern media, which is 24/7 and often personality driven, the personality of Prime Minister has become ever more important. Prime Ministers have always had to be dominant, confident individuals but as the monarch plays no political role, the Prime Minister has to speak for the country both at home and abroad.

Unlike the Prime Minister, the First Minister is elected by all the MSPs, not just by members of his own party. In reality, as with Westminster, the party with the most MSPs will normally be in a position to nominate their leader as First Minister and the election of First Minister will be a formality. Like the First Minister, he/she is then appointed by the monarch.

The main role of the First Minister is to represent Scotland in the areas that are reserved to the Scottish Parliament. The First Minister is expected to have a vision for the country and to lead the country in a positive direction.

Like the Prime Minister, he is the leader of the Cabinet. He/she selects the MSPs he feels are best to lead the country to the Scottish Cabinet.

The First Minister is accountable to the Scottish Parliament. He/she must appear at First Minister's Question Time to answer questions from MSPs.

The First Minister will often represent Scotland at an international level. Scotland has many natural resources, such as oil, gas and fishing which the nation can exploit. Tourism is important to Scotland; many thousands of people wish to visit Scotland to take in the nation's history, islands, hills and golf courses. Scotland is a world leader in the export of whisky. The First Minister is therefore often busy promoting Scotland as a place to visit and do business with.

In this respect, some of his work can overlap with the UK Secretary of State for Scotland.

Prior to devolution, the Secretary of State for Scotland was Scotland's voice at home and abroad. Today, the Secretary of State for Scotland continues to represent Scotland at a UK level in the UK Cabinet.

He represents Scotland in issues that reserved to Westminster, such as defence and foreign affairs.

THE SCOTTISH PARLIAMENT

The Scotland Act 1998 created the Scottish Parliament. Unless the people of Scotland vote otherwise in an Independence Referendum, Scotland remains part of the United Kingdom. When a new Scottish Parliament opens, the newly elected MSPs swear allegiance to the Queen. Like Westminster, all Bills passed by the Scottish Parliament have to receive the Royal Assent by the monarch before they can become law.

The UK Parliament has evolved over the centuries. By contrast, in 1999, Scotland had the chance to start a new Parliament, looking all over the world at the most democratic ways of running a country.

There are four principles which guide the work of the Scottish Parliament.

PRINCIPLE ONE: SHARING POWER

"The Scottish Parliament should embody and reflect the sharing of power between the people of Scotland, the legislators and the Scottish Government."

The Scottish Parliament has 129 members, usually referred to as MSPs. 73 of these MSPs represent constituencies in the same way as MPs represent constituencies in the House of Commons. An additional 56 MSPs represent wider regional constituencies. This is because the Scottish Parliament has a voting system called the Additional Member System (AMS). AMS tries to elect a more proportional set of MSPs than the First Past the Post system the Commons uses. Sometimes a political party can win a good share of the vote but have no representatives elected. AMS tries to redress this problem by allowing voters to vote twice; once for their constituency MSP and then again, for a regional MSP.

The creators of the Scottish Parliament hoped that this voting system would result in a more diverse set of MSPs elected, allowing parties who had some support in the country to have a voice in parliament. The Scottish Greens have been successful in having MSPs elected. Likewise, in the past, the Scottish Socialist Party had some MSPs elected.

PRINCIPLE TWO: ACCOUNTABILITY

"The Scottish Government should be accountable to the Scottish Parliament and the Parliament and executive should be accountable to the people of Scotland."

Parliamentary procedures, such as First Minister's Question Time and powerful committees are designed to hold the Scottish Government to account.

The Scottish Parliament has a Presiding Officer whose role is comparable to that of the Speaker in the Commons. He/she is to be neutral to MSPs of all parties, making sure that parliamentary business is carried out efficiently and fairly.

The Scottish Parliament has no House of Lords to check its work. Instead, it has a powerful committee system, which can propose as well as scrutinise bills. In the committees, MSPs discuss legislation in detail and work closely together.

A body called the Parliamentary Bureau proposes which MSPs should be on the committees, as well as which parties should hold the convenorship of the committees. The proposals then have to be approved at a meeting of the whole Parliament. (The Parliamentary Bureau is chaired by the Presiding Officer and has representatives of each party with five or more MSPs).

Members are selected with regard to the balance of political parties in the Parliament.

PRINCIPLE THREE: ACCESS AND PARTICIPATION

The Scottish Parliament should be:

"Accessible, open, responsive and develop procedures which make possible a participative approach to the development, consideration and scrutiny of policy and legislation."

While the Scottish Parliament is located in Edinburgh, the Scottish Cabinet visits locations elsewhere in Scotland during each summer.

Since 2008, more than 4,000 people have taken part in Summer Cabinet events in Dundee, Melrose, Stornoway, Aberdeen, Glasgow, Dumfries, Inverness, Pitlochry, Skye, Isle of Bute, Dornoch, Stirling and Kilmarnock.

Additionally, some of the Scottish Parliament's committee meetings have been held outside of Edinburgh to allow greater public access and participation.

The Scottish Parliament offers ordinary citizens the chance to engage with members of the Scottish parliament.

The Scottish Parliament's Public Petitions Committee considers any issues raised by members of the public brought to the Scottish Parliament in the form of a petition, providing they meet certain criteria.

PRINCIPLE FOUR: EQUAL OPPORTUNITIES

"The Scottish Parliament in its operation and its appointments should recognise the need to promote equal opportunities for all."

The opening hours of Scottish Parliament were designed to help MSPs with family

24

commitments and are regarded by many as leading to greater numbers of female MSPs. Since 1999, around one third of MSPs have been female, a higher percentage than the Commons, where around one fifth of MPs are female.

LEARNING ACTIVITY: PRINCIPLES OF THE SCOTTISH PARLIAMENT

Make a spider diagram which shows the four founding principles of the Scottish Parliament.

Explain, in detail if possible, how successful the Scottish Parliament has been in meeting these founding principles.

POWERS OF THE SCOTTISH PARLIAMENT

The Scottish Parliament Is funded by an annual budget from the UK Parliament of around £30 billion. The Scottish Parliament has the power to make laws on a range of 'devolved' issues. These powers were extended by the Scotland Act 2012.

Other powers are 'reserved' to the UK Parliament.

Devolved Powers (Scotland)	Reserved Powers (UK)
Health	· Constitutional Matters
Education	· Defence
Social Work	· Some Transport
Planning	· Social Security
Economic development	· Data Protection
Courts and legal system	· Equal Opportunities
Environment	· UK Foreign Policy
Local Government	· National Security
Housing	· Trade and Industry
Tourism	· Employment Law
Some Transport	· Gambling and National Lottery
Police and Fire Services	· Abortion
Agriculture, forestry & fishing	· Broadcasting/ Entertainment
Public Registers and Records Natural and built heritage	· Drug Laws · Elections
Sport and the Arts	
Legislation on	
air guns*	
drink–driving*	
speeding limits*	
stamp duty*	
land tax and landfill tax*	
(*from Scotland Act 2012)	

As a result of the Scotland Act 2012, the Scottish Parliament can introduce a Scottish rate of income tax and have borrowing powers of up to £5bn. These powers will not come into effect until 2016.

LEARNING ACTIVITY: DEVOLUTION

In groups, make a poster that highlights the powers which the Scottish Parliament and UK Parliament.

Try to find any newspaper/website articles you can find to illustrate some of the powers. Stick these on to your poster to illustrate your understanding.

LOCAL COUNCILS

All the nations within the UK have a system of local government.

Councils make and carry out decisions on local services such as transport, education, planning, social care, libraries, fire and public safety and waste management.

Local councilors are elected by the local community to represent views. Each council is made up of councllors who are directly elected by the residents In the population of the area they represent.

THE MONARCHY

The UK's political system can be described as a constitutional monarchy. This means that we have a king or queen as our Head of State.

However, the two houses of Parliament make our laws, not the monarch. The monarch only formally passes legislation. This is called giving the Royal Assent. The Monarch must remain politically neutral and does not interfere with the legislative process. No monarch has refused Parliament's wishes for over 300 years. Some people, however, question how neutral the monarchy is. In December 2012 The Guardian newspaper revealed that Prince Charles had held private meetings with eight government ministers during 2012. No ordinary citizen could have this access to Government.

When a Bill is given Royal Assent it becomes an Act of Parliament. It is then up to the relevant government department to implement that law (e.g. the Transport department will deal with new Acts relating to transport).

Strictly speaking, the Prime Minister must ask the monarch's permission if he can hold a general election. After a general election, the monarch asks the leader of the party with most MPs if he or she thinks they could form a government. Constitutionally, it is his/her Majesty's Government. In theory, if the general election doesn't produce a clear winner, the monarch might have to decide which party leader will be in charge.

The monarch opens a new session of Parliament. The monarch goes to the House of Lords, because since the 17th century, the monarch has been barred from entering the House of Commons.

The monarch reads 'The Queen's Speech', which announces what the government plans to do in the coming year. The Prime Minister writes the speech for her.

Not all countries have monarchies. The United States, for example, is the most famous example of a Republic, where there is an elected head of state. In the UK, the monarch's role in the governing of the UK is largely a symbolic one. The monarch has no real political power. Instead the monarch symbolizes what the country stands for.

This is where people disagree over the monarchy. Some people do not like what the monarchy stands for. They would like the UK to be a constitutional Republic where the head of state is elected and therefore, represents a different set of values.

LEARNING ACTIVITY: THE MONARCHY

You are a researcher working for a political party. You have been asked to research the issue of whether the UK should replace the monarchy with a Republic. You are to produce a PowerPoint presentation which outlines the key arguments and comes to a decision on which form of government you think would be best for the UK.

- **In your PowerPoint you must make a clear decision.**

- **You must use evidence from the sources to support your decision.**

- **You must say why you did not choose the other option.**

In your PowerPoint you must also show your knowledge and understanding of the work of the monarchy in the UK system of government.

- **Describe the work of the monarchy in the UK system of government.**

- **Explain the reasons for having a monarchy.**

SOURCE 1 VIEWS ON THE MONARCHY

Pro Monarchy www.royal.gov.uk	Pro Republic www.republic.org.uk
The monarchy is our link to the past and to the traditions of the UK. It is better to have a head of state who is non-party political and above political squabbling. The UK monarchy has evolved and is highly relevant to the modern world. The monarchy adds glamour and excitement to the lives of many people and organisations.	The monarchy is outdated and a relic of a bygone age when ordinary people believed certain people to be superior. The monarchy symbolises inherited wealth, which has no place in modern society. People should get their rewards through their own efforts. Abolishing the monarchy will need a new constitution. This will provide a chance to make sure that everyone in power in the UK is elected by the people.

SOURCE 2 OPINION POLL, GLASGOW 2013

Do you think the UK should have an elected head of state?

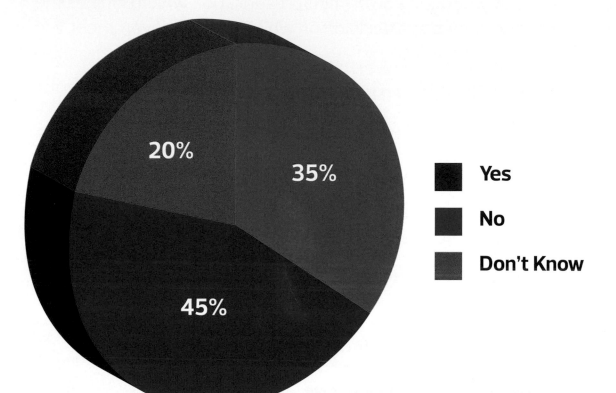

■	Yes
■	No
■	Don't Know

SOURCE 3 G8 COUNTRIES AND FORM OF GOVERNMENT

COUNTRY	FORM OF GOVERNMENT
Canada	Constitutional Monarchy
France	Republic
Germany	Republic
Italy	Republic
Japan	Constitutional Monarchy
Russia	Republic
United Kingdom	Constitutional Monarchy
United States	Republic

SOURCE 4 FACTFILE ON THE UK MONARCHY

The Queen carries out around 400 engagements a year, to meet people, open events and buildings, unveil plaques and make speeches.

The Queen visits a wide variety of organisations, including schools, hospitals, factories, military units, art galleries, sheltered accommodation for elderly people, hostels for the homeless, local community schemes in inner city areas, and other British and Commonwealth organisations.

The Queen's official expenditure totaled £32.3m in 2011/12. The figure does not include the cost of security and protection.

Travel undertaken by the Duke of York cost a total of £358,000. These included an £81,000 visit to Saudi Arabia, and a trip to Thailand, Malaysia and China that cost £72,000.

The tax arrangements for the Queen and the Prince of Wales are the same as for any other taxpayer. They pay income tax and capital gains tax.

The 1701 Act of Settlement excludes Roman Catholics, Muslims and other non-Protestants from succeeding to the throne. The Treason Felony Act of 1848 makes it an offence to intend to abolish the monarchy.

THE INDEPENDENCE DEBATE

The United Kingdom of England, Scotland, Northern Ireland and Wales has not always existed. There have always been tensions within the Union.

Wales was brought under English control by the Laws in Wales Acts 1535 and 1542. Scotland was an independent nation until the Union of the Crowns in 1707. Northern Ireland as country only came into creation in 1922 after the Republic of Ireland became an independent state.

Since then, within each nation, there have been demands for reform of how the UK is governed. Sometimes powerful and popular demands for independence.

In Northern Ireland, national identity and relations with the UK have resulted in violence. The Good Friday Agreement of 1998 has resulted in more democratic ways of resolving national tensions.

Thankfully, the national question in Scotland has rarely resulted in political violence. After the Union of the Crowns, Scotland retained its own education and legal systems, meaning that Scotland always had some control over some important aspects of life.

However, growing differences in political allegiances, in part linked to the differing living standards of England and Scotland, resulted in the creation of the modern Scottish Parliament in 1999. This process, called devolution, was an attempt by the Westminster government to modernise the United Kingdom by giving each nation some decision making powers at its own national level.

Since 1999, Scottish Governments at the Holyrood Scottish Parliament have pursued social/economic policies which have been different from England. Some of these, such as the ban in smoking in enclosed public places, the ending of prescription charges and the promise of no university tuition fees have been hailed as Scottish ways of doing things. To supporters of independence, they are evidence that if the Scottish Parliament could have full powers, Scotland could become an even better country.

By contrast, those who oppose Scottish independence argue that Scotland is better remaining within the United Kingdom. Independence, they argue, is simply unnecessary and potentially destructive.

YOUR SCOTLAND, YOUR REFERENDUM

Autumn 2014

www.scotreferendum.com

The Scottish Government

Views of Scottish Independence supporters	Views of Scotland within the UK supporters
www.yesscotland.net	www.bettertogether.net
Independence will bring more confidence and responsibility to all living in Scotland.	The UK is better placed than a separate Scotland to help Scottish businesses win orders across the world.
Scotland has the resources; natural, human and economic to be a prosperous country.	Scotland is a more secure country protected by the UK armed forces.
Only the full tax raising powers of independence can allow Scotland to improve schools and hospitals in the ways they need.	Independence will bring uncertainty and instability which is bad for business.
An independent Scotland will get rid of nuclear weapons. The billions saved can be spent on public services.	The current Scottish Parliament has many powers. These, combined, with the security of the UK, give Scotland the best of both worlds.

LEARNING ACTIVITY: SCOTTISH INDEPENDENCE

Read over the above arguments both for and against Scottish independence.

Look up the websites for the respective 'for' and 'against' pressure groups.

Describe, in detail, if you can, the arguments for and against Scottish independence.

How would you vote in a referendum on Scottish independence?

Justify your decision with evidence and/or examples.
Why is your choice the better of the two options?

Chapter Two:
Skills and Knowledge

Democracy in Scotland

The following information illustrates the skills and knowledge that will be assessed within the Democracy in Scotland and the United Kingdom unit of National 4 and National 5 Modern Studies. This does not mean that you will not use the other skills that Modern Studies develops. Remember also that you will be assessed in these other skills in the other two units (Social Issues in the United Kingdom and International Issues) and in the Added Value of your course.

N4: Modern Studies Skills and Knowledge

- Detecting bias and/or exaggeration using two sources of information

- Briefly explaining bias and/or exaggeration using evidence from two sources of information

- Giving straightforward descriptions of the main features of a political issue, from either Democracy in Scotland and/or the United Kingdom

- Giving straightforward explanations relating to a political issue in Scotland and/or the United Kingdom

N5: Modern Studies Skills and Knowledge

- Detecting exaggeration and/or selective use of facts using at least two and no more than four sources of information

- Explaining, in detail, exaggeration and/or selective use of facts using evidence from these sources of information

- Giving detailed descriptions of a political issue that show theoretical and factual knowledge of Democracy in Scotland and/or the United Kingdom

- Giving detailed explanations relating to a political issue in Scotland and/or the United Kingdom

SCOTTISH PARLIAMENT COMMITTEES

Unlike the Westminster Parliament, the Scottish Parliament has no second chamber to scrutinise legislation in detail. In the Scottish Parliament this work is carried out by committees.

The Scottish Parliament has a number of committees that MSPs can join. These are 'mandatory' committees, which the Scottish Parliament must have, such as the Equal Opportunities committee and the Finance committee. The other type of committee is a 'Subject' committee which can be set up by the Scottish government of the day. Current examples include the Education and Culture committee and the Health and Sport committee.

Committees have between five and fifteen members, with their make-up based on the proportion of seats each party has overall. It is often claimed that the committees are where the real work of the Parliament is done. MSPs discuss legislation in real detail and work more closely together. MSPs are more likely to discuss issues on their merits rather than oppose them on a party political basis.

The committees have the power to require anyone, including Scottish Government Ministers, to give evidence before them and to produce documents in connection with their inquiries.

Committees meet weekly or fortnightly, usually on Tuesdays or on Wednesday mornings, in one of the Scottish Parliament's committee rooms.

Most committee meetings are open to the public and often, in the summer, many go outside of the parliament and meet across Scotland.

Unlike Westminster, Scottish Parliament committees can propose, as well as scrutinise legislation.

THE WORK OF AN MSP

The Scottish Parliament has 129 members, usually referred to as MSPs. 73 of these MSPs represent constituencies in the same way as MPs represent constituencies for the House of Commons. An additional 56 MSPs represent wider regional constituencies. This is because the Scottish Parliament has a voting system called the Additional Member System (AMS).

AMS tries to elect a more proportional set of MSPs than the First Past the Post system the Commons uses. Sometimes a political party can win a good share of the vote but have no representatives elected. AMS tries to address this problem by allowing voters to vote twice; once for their constituency MSP and then again, for a regional MSP.

Voters in Scotland, therefore have eight potential MSPs (one constituency and seven regional list) they can contact regarding any of the devolved powers.

MSPs can represent their constituents in a number of ways, including:

- **Writing to or meeting with a relevant Cabinet Secretary or Minister**

- **Speaking in the Parliament during debates**

- **Asking questions during First Minister's Questions (FMQs)**

- **Introducing Members Bills on topics of concern to their constituents**

- **Lobbying other organisations (such as local councils, health boards) and individuals on behalf of their constituents**

- **Raising the profile of an issue in the media**

Humza Yousaf MSP

Born: 7 April 1985

Educated: Hutcheson's Grammar School, Glasgow, University of Glasgow.

Party: Scottish National Party

Represents: Glasgow

Interests: Tackling poverty, civil liberties, equality and Scotland's role in the global world.

In September 2012, Humza was appointed Minister for External Affairs and International Development in September 2012. Responsibilities include external affairs, international development, culture and the arts, broadcasting, architecture, built heritage, Historic Scotland and lottery funding, National Records of Scotland and major events strategy.

A TYPICAL DIARY OF AN MSP WOULD BE...

Most MSPs sit on at least one Scottish Parliament committee, where they scrutinise bills.

Cross Party Committee groups cover a wide range of topics and are vital in holding the Government to account.

MONDAY
Constituency day

- Surgery held in the office
- Staff meeting
- Visit local school
- Party meeting

TUESDAY

- Scottish Parliament Committee meeting
- Attend debate in the main Scottish Parliament chamber
- Appointment with constituent

WEDNESDAY

- Scottish Parliament Committee meeting
- Meeting with national charity
- Staff meeting
- Attend evening function at Scottish Parliament

THURSDAY

- Briefing meeting for First Minister's Questions
- Scottish Parliament Question Time
- First Minister's Questions

FRIDAY

- Constituency day
- Surgery at local library
- Many gala days in the summer
- In winter often speeches at community centre or other local meeting

Constituents are a very diverse group! The MSP has to represent all his/her constituents, regardless of whether or not they voted for him/her

SATURDAY

- Visit local sports complex
- Surgery at community centre
- Speaking at local business dinner

Most MSPs have their own website. Many MSPs are now using social media to inform constituents of their work

SUNDAY

- Meeting constituents at various locations around Glasgow
- Lunch followed by Questions and Answer session at pensioners club

LEARNING ACTIVITY: THE WORK OF AN MSP

Imagine you are the MSP for your constituency:

http://www.scottish.parliament.uk/msps/177.aspx

You can either be a constituency MSP or an MSP from your regional list.

You can be a member of any political party you choose.

Design a Twitter feed for your typical week.

Think of issues that have been going on in your constituency and the Scottish Parliament.

VOTING AND THE ADDITIONAL MEMBER SYSTEM

The Additional Member System (AMS) is a 'hybrid' system of voting, containing an element of the First Past The Post (FPTP) voting system used for elections to the House of Commons and a proportional element. It can therefore be seen as a compromise between the FPTP and proportional systems.

Ruth Davidson MSP

The founders of the Scottish Parliament believed that under the AMS, it would take exceptional circumstances for any one party to win an overall majority in the Scottish Parliament. Yet, in 2011 the SNP won a total of 69 out of the 129 seats, giving it an overall majority.

The first two Scottish elections, in 1999 and 2003 resulted in 'hung parliaments'. This is where one party has the largest number of MSPs, but does not have an overall majority.

In these elections Scottish Labour won the most votes and the most MSPs but did not have an overall majority of MSPs. It therefore chose to enter into coalitions with the Scottish Liberal Democrats in order to have as many of its policies passed as possible. In some cases it had to compromise.

This is what happens in 'coalition politics'. In 2007, the SNP won the most votes and the most seats. It was unable to obtain an overall majority of MSPs over the other political parties. Unlike Scottish Labour though, the SNP decided to 'go it alone' as a minority Government, winning support for its legislation on an 'issue by issue' basis.

At Scottish Parliament elections each voter has two votes:

- **The first vote elects a constituency MSP**

- **The second vote is used to elect additional seven 'list' MSPs**

Electing a Constituency MSP	Electing a List MSP
There are 73 constituencies in Scotland. Each constituency in Scotland is represented by one constituency MSP.	Scotland is divided into eight regions.
The First Past the Post system (FPTP) is used to elect the constituency MSP.	Each region is represented by seven constituency MSPs.
The voter places an 'X' next to their candidate of choice. The candidate with the most votes is elected as the constituency MSP.	The voter places an 'X' next to their preferred political party. The percentage of votes that each of the parties receives dictates how many candidates from that party become MSPs.

Voters can vote for a different party in the list election than the one they voted for in the first, FPTP election. Or, they can vote for the same party in both.

This system means that each voter in Scotland, therefore, has a total of eight MSPs he/she could contact about issues the Scottish Parliament has control over.

AMS Advantages	AMS Disadvantages
The AMS is a compromise. It is the best of the FPTP system and the best of a proportional system. Parties who win a reasonable amount of votes will be rewarded with some representation.	AMS is not truly proportional. This is unfair in modern party politics as most voters vote for parties not individuals. Parties should get the same percentage of seats as they get in votes.
The FPTP constituency part enables there to be a local MSP who the voters have decided should be the constituency MSP for that area.	If there a constituency MSP, surely the other MSPs are seen as lesser, 'compensation' MSPs rather than the real thing?
The AMS provides voters with a choice of representative to go to. In Scotland, the voter has one constituency and seven regional MSPs. For most people, there will be a variety of political parties and a choice of male or female MSP to go to.	In the FPTP constituency vote of the AMS election there are many "safe" seats where most voters know who will win before the campaign starts. This is unfair as those who vote for opposition parties have no incentive to vote at all as their vote will be wasted.

A MORE PROPORTIONAL SYSTEM?

The Single Transferable Voting system is used for elections to Scottish local councils.

Here, there are larger constituencies (called 'wards' in Scottish local councils). Instead of placing one 'X' next to the one candidate of choice, voters can rank candidates 1, 2, 3, 4 etc.

In STV, it is more complicated working out who gets elected. But this is done by computer software. In deciding who gets elected, the number of first preference votes a candidate receives is calculated. Candidates who reach a certain 'quota' of votes, based on the voting population and how many candidates, are elected.

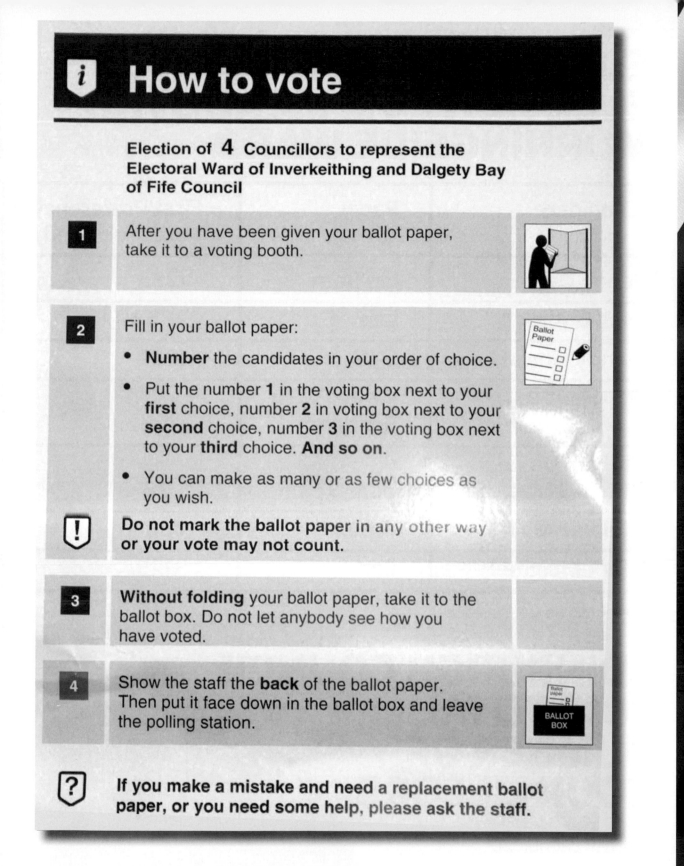

How to vote

Election of **4** Councillors to represent the Electoral Ward of Inverkeithing and Dalgety Bay of Fife Council

1 After you have been given your ballot paper, take it to a voting booth.

2 Fill in your ballot paper:

- **Number** the candidates in your order of choice.

- Put the number **1** in the voting box next to your **first** choice, number **2** in voting box next to your **second** choice, number **3** in the voting box next to your **third** choice. **And so on.**

- You can make as many or as few choices as you wish.

Do not mark the ballot paper in any other way or your vote may not count.

3 **Without folding** your ballot paper, take it to the ballot box. Do not let anybody see how you have voted.

4 Show the staff the **back** of the ballot paper. Then put it face down in the ballot box and leave the polling station.

If you make a mistake and need a replacement ballot paper, or you need some help, please ask the staff.

Overall, STV tends to provide a more proportional result. Unlike FPTP, voters don't have to 'put all their eggs in one basket'. They may like more than one candidate and can reflect this in how they vote. Parties also can stand more than one candidate if they wish.

Depending on the voting population of the ward, voters will have a number of representatives.

Here is an example from the Meadows and Morningside ward in Edinburgh City Council, where four candidates are elected.

EDINBURGH CITY COUNCIL ELECTION 2012 MEADOWS/ MORNINGSIDE WARD

Candidate	Party	First Preference Votes received
Jenny Dawe	Lib Dem	1285
Paul Godzik *	Lab	2053
Sandy Howat*	SNP	1650
Phil Hunt	Pirate Party Scotland	195
William David Mitchell MacAdam	UKIP	79
Melanie Main*	Green	2064
Mark McInnes*	Con	3125

* = elected as Councillor

EDINBURGH COUNCIL 2012 TOTAL NUMBER OF COUNCILLORS

Scottish Labour: 20

Scottish National Party: 18

Scottish Conservatives: 11

Scottish Green Party: 6

Scottish Liberal Democrats: 3

EDINBURGH COUNCIL 2012 PERCENTAGE OF VOTES BY PARTY

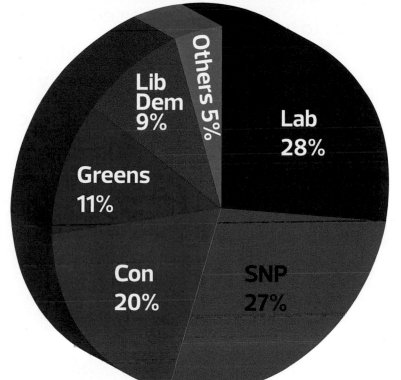

EDINBURGH COUNCIL 2012 PERCENTAGE OF COUNCILLORS BY PARTY

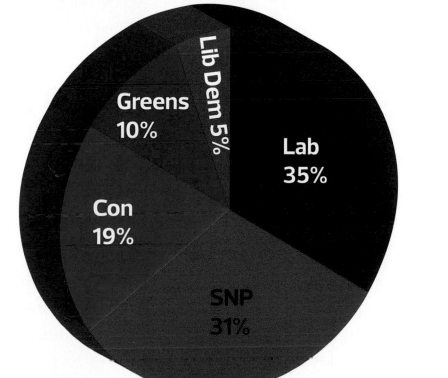

45

STV Advantages	STV Disadvantages
Voters can vote for more than one candidate.	Voters have more than one representative, could be confused who to speak to.
Overall result tends to be more proportional.	Voters could be confused as to who is actually in charge.
There are no safe seats, every vote counts.	Voters could be confused who to vote for.

LEARNING ACTIVITY: EXTENDED WRITING ON VOTING SYSTEMS

- Decide whether you think the AMS should be replaced by a more proportional voting system, such as the Single Transferable Vote.

- Explain your argument in detail, if possible, using evidence and examples.

- Justify why you think the your voting system is the fairest.

- Write your arguments in the form of a letter to a newspaper.

THE MEDIA AND THE 2011 SCOTTISH ELECTIONS

The media plays a powerful role in our democracy. It is no surprise that countries which do not have a democratic system, such as China, have a Government which strictly controls what its population can read and hear.

The UK has always been proud of its traditions of freedom of speech, freedom to express a point of point of view and the freedom to publish points of view be it in newspapers, books, magazines, radio and increasingly these days, online.

With these rights come responsibilities. The laws of slander mean that a person or organization can be taken in court for making harmful or untrue statements about someone else/another organisation. The laws of libel mean a person or organization can be taken to court for publishing harmful or untrue statements about someone else/another organization. The laws of libel apply to online communication; websites, blogs and social media too not just the print media. There are many examples of people/organisations being successfully sued for making inaccurate or damaging accusations.

By law, television organisations must provide balanced and unbiased coverage of political events. They are not supposed to favour any one political party or point of view. News programmes, for example on BBC or the commercial channels must hold the Government to account by asking challenging questions. They must have spokespersons from different points of view.

By contrast, the print media; be it newspapers or online, can be as biased as it likes. Newspapers are free to support any political party, cause or viewpoint. British newspapers have traditions of supporting a political party. Indeed some people may choose to buy a newspaper because of its overall political approach.

There are differences between 'quality' newspapers and tabloids. Examples of 'quality' newspapers are The Guardian, The Independent, The Times, The Daily Telegraph, or here in Scotland, The Herald and The Scotsman. These newspapers contain a lot of political news. They cover news stories, at home and abroad, in detail. They usually attempt to be unbiased and cover differing points of view. They normally support a political party or certain social/moral viewpoints. But they show this in a special section called 'The Editorial', which is a column where it explains what it thinks about a particular issue.

On the other hand, the tabloids (or 'red tops') can sometimes be much more aggressive and biased in their reporting of political issues. Examples of tabloids are The Sun, The Daily Express, The Daily Mail and, in Scotland, the Scottish version of The Sun and the Daily Record. Tabloids often campaign against a particular issue, devoting big headlines attacking the Government or individuals. While they devote a lot of space to stories about celebrities and sport, they are also highly political. Their stories are often emotive, focusing on real life human experiences rather than the political process. At election time tabloid newspapers are frequently very biased in favour or against a political party.

They can show their support in a number of ways. They can include good news stories about the party they support. They can publish bad news stories about the parties they do not support. They can show flattering photographs of the leader they support. They can publish unflattering images of the leaders they do not like. They can run sustained campaigns of 'propaganda' where they 'drip drip' good news about the party support and bad news about the parties they do not. In the run up to election day itself, many pages can be devoted to biased coverage, including 'pull out' sections packed with images and loaded political messages.

But, the media world is changing. There are numerous TV channels with multiple news programmes on 24/7. Sales of national newspapers have been in decline for a number of years. Many working people find it difficult to find the time to read, especially read quality newspapers. 'Free' newspapers such The Metro, with its 'chunks' of news offer an alternative to commuters to buying a daily newspaper. Many people can now get their news online for free. Twitter, especially, carries news instantly and allows people to comment and/or communicate with newsmakers directly.

LEARNING ACTIVITY: NEWSPAPERS/DIGITAL MEDIA

Create your own newspaper front/blog post on the 2011 Scottish elections outcome.

Decide which political party you support and 'spin' the information to make the outcome as positive as possible for your favourite.

Provide your account of how the 2011 Scottish elections went.

Without telling any lies or making up stories, it should contain the best possible news for your favourite, describing and explaining the most encouraging aspects of the campaign and the results.

2011 SCOTTISH PARLIAMENT ELECTION

The 2011 Scottish election was truly historic. Most people believed that no party could win an overall majority in the Scottish Parliament under the AMS. But the SNP did. It won both the majority of votes and the majority of seats.

In the aftermath of the election, the leaders of the Scottish Conservatives, Scottish Labour and Scottish Liberal Democrats resigned as their parties grappled with how to beat the SNP, and in particular, its leader, Alex Salmond.

Like the UK General election, there were televised debates between the party leaders. However, unlike in the UK election, no party leader appeared to dominate. It was widely agreed that no one leader landed any 'knock out punches'. However, SNP leader Alex Salmond was by far the better known and the SNP campaigned strongly on his qualities to be First Minister if the SNP were to be re-elected as the Government of Scotland.

While the television media has to remain neutral, one game-changing televised moment did occur. Labour leader Iain Gray was televised running away from a protestor in Glasgow into a sandwich shop. The incident was televised on news programmes and 'went viral' via YouTube and social networks. The coverage was not positive for Mr Gray and was good news for the SNP campaign.

SOURCE 1 OPINION POLL PUBLIC RECOGNITION OF PARTY LEADERS

Can you name the leader of the following political parties?

Party Leader	Percentage of Public who recognise leader
Alex Salmond (SNP)	84%
Annabel Goldie (Scottish Conservatives)	36%
Iain Gray (Scottish Labour)	26%
Tavish Scott (Scottish Liberal Democrats)	18%

"All the Scottish party leaders are equally well-known." **Paula Heaton**

What evidence is there that Paula Heaton is exaggerating?

SOURCE 2: SEATS WON BY PARTY

	Constituency Seats	Regional List Seats	Total Seats
SNP	53	16	69
Scottish Labour	15	22	37
Scottish Conservatives	3	12	15
Scottish Liberal Democrats	2	3	5
Scottish Greens	0	2	2
Independent	0	1	1

The SNP capitalised on leader Alex Salmond's popularity during the election campaign

51

SOURCE 3: PERCENTAGE OF VOTES WON BY PARTY (CONSTITUENCY VOTE)

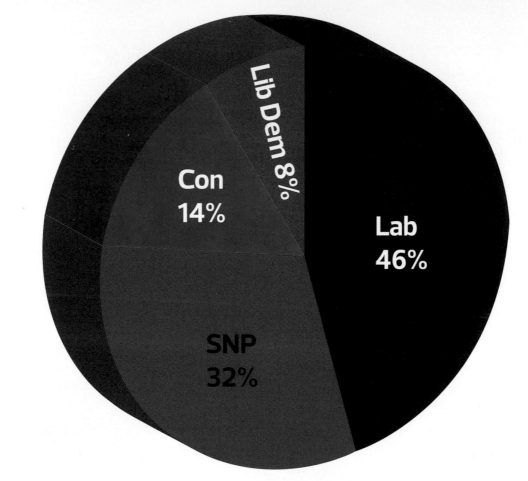

Lib Dem 8%

Con 14%

Lab 46%

SNP 32%

SOURCE 4: VOTING INTENTIONS BY SOCIAL CLASS AND GENDER

Party	Working Class	Middle Class	Female	Male
SNP	46%	38%	44%	46%
Scottish Labour	34%	16%	28%	25%
Scottish Conservatives	7%	23%	11%	13%
Scottish Liberal Democrats	5%	7%	6%	5%
Scottish Greens	4%	10%	4%	5%
Others	6%	6%	7%	6%

The 2011 Scottish election result was a triumph for the SNP. Labour used to do well in constituency seats but now the SNP is winning most constituency seats. The SNP also won the majority of constituency votes. Across all social classes and genders, the SNP was the most popular party.

View of Jim Burchill

Using sources 2, 3 and 4, explain in detail, if you can, the extent to which Jim Burchill could be accused of being selective in the use of facts.

THE PRESS

In 2007, the SNP won the Scottish election without the support of the most popular newspapers. So, the influence of the press on election outcomes can be exaggerated.

However, there is no doubt that political parties would like to have the press on their side. In 2011, of the daily newspapers available in Scotland, The Scottish Sun decided to support the SNP (but not the SNP's support for Scottish independence). The SNP cleverly decided that a vote for the SNP was not necessarily a vote for Scottish independence. If elected, the SNP would provide a referendum on Scottish independence in which the Scottish voters could decide if they wanted independence to happen.

The News of the World, The Scotsman, The Scotland on Sunday, The Sunday Herald and The Scottish Sunday Express all supported the SNP too.

The Daily Record backed Scottish Labour.

PARTY POLICIES

At modern General Elections, the major political parties like to highlight the personal qualities of their leader, emphasising his/her qualities to be a good Prime Minister.

The parties publish their policies in a 'manifesto'. This is their 'contract' with the voters should they be elected to form a Government. Few voters actually read the manifesto though. Most will form their opinion of the party from what they see in the media; either through the TV news or newspapers. Sometimes voters will watch a party election broadcast. Increasingly the parties are using the new media of Facebook and Twitter to get across their 'big idea'. The big idea is each party's vision of what it wants to do should it be elected. It is the one idea it wants voters to remember.

SCOTTISH CONSERVATIVES BIG IDEA: 'COMMON SENSE FOR SCOTLAND'

The Scottish Conservatives campaigned on the idea that there are certain 'common sense' solutions to Scotland's social/economic challenges.

It believed that the public would respond to straightforward, practical solutions.

So, policies included:

- encouraging parents and charities to set up new academy schools
- giving people the power to veto council tax rises through local referendums
- promising communities the right to buy their local pub or post office

  The Scottish Conservatives promised
- Introduce variable university graduate fee, capped at £4,000
- More police officers
- End automatic early release from prison
- Freeze on Council Tax increases for next 2 years and a £200 council tax cut for every pensioner household
- Reduce school leaving age to 14, provided pupils sign up to a monitored apprenticeship or a full-time vocational or technical training course

SCOTTISH GREENS BIG IDEA 'PROTECT THE ENVIRONMENT FOR EVERYONE'

The Scottish Greens did not believe it could win the election. After all, it was only standing in the regional list election where it knew it had a chance of winning some representation. It hoped to hold the balance of power if no one party had an overall majority. It would, therefore, be in a position to move the Scottish Government towards more 'greener', environmentally aware policies.

So, policies included:

- No tuition fees for Scottish students at Scottish universities
- Support minimum pricing of alcohol
- Scrap the Aberdeen West Peripheral Route and new Forth road bridge, while repairing the existing one
- Close existing nuclear power stations at or before the end of their normal working lives
- Focus on crime prevention

55

SCOTTISH LABOUR BIG IDEA

Scottish Labour's "big idea" was that Scottish Labour was the only party with costed, affordable policies. It campaigned negatively on the SNP Government's record, claiming that the SNP had broken promises on spending on public services and that a vote for the SNP meant breaking up Britain.

So, policies included:

- No tuition fees for Scottish students at Scottish universities

- Specialised training for up to 1,000 teachers, to boost literacy and numeracy standards;

- Give every young person right to quality training, stay in school or to go into further education until they are 18, by 2015

- Six-month mandatory minimum jail sentence for carrying knife

- Reinstate Glasgow Airport Rail Link

SCOTTISH LIBERAL DEMOCRATS BIG IDEA: 'FAIRNESS'

The Liberal Democrats' "big idea" was fairness; it claimed to be the only party' who would be fair in the economic and political changes Scotland requires.

So, policies included:

- No tuition fees for Scottish students at Scottish universities

- £250m early years intervention fund

- Provide opportunity for youngsters to attend college to do a course of their choice from the age of 14

- Put dual lanes on the A9 to Inverness

- Superfast broadband in all parts of Scotland

SCOTTISH NATIONAL PARTY BIG IDEA: 'LET'S MAKE SCOTLAND BETTER'

The SNP put party leader Alex Salmond at the centre of its campaign. He featured in all campaign leaflets, posters and election broadcasts. The SNP even put his name at the top of the regional list ballot paper, asking voters to vote 'Alex Salmond for First Minister.'

So, policies included:

- No tuition fees for Scottish students at Scottish universities

- A referendum for Scottish independence

- A freeze on Council Tax increases

- Edinburgh–Glasgow rail electrification

- Take forward infrastructure projects including Borders Railway and M8 Baillieston to Newhouse, M74 Raith Junction and M8, M73 and M74 network improvements

LEARNING ACTIVITY: MOCK ELECTION

Adopt one of the major political parties (or a smaller one such as UKIP or the Green Party).

You will be able to find their most up to date policies on the respective party websites:

www.conservatives.com

www.greenparty.org.uk

www.labour.org.uk

www.libdems.org.uk

www.snp.org

www.ukip.org

You could make:

- Posters
- Leaflets
- Badges
- An election broadcast
- A blog page
- A website home page

You should divide up the jobs between members of your group, giving everyone something meaningful to do.

In all your communications you should include:

Your party branding; party logo, making sure your colours are coordinated in your party's colours.

Your big idea which you want to get across to the voters. You can also have 'negative' messages about the other parties (but not negative messages about your fellow learners in those groups!)

LOCAL COUNCILS IN SCOTLAND

There are 32 local councils in Scotland. Some, such as Highland and Glasgow are very different in terms of their size, population and social/economic needs. But others, particularly neighbouring ones, such as East and North Ayrshire, are quite similar in size, population and social/economic needs.

Roles of Local Councils in Scotland

Providing Services. Local councils provide vital services such as education, housing, parks, refuse disposal and social work, services many people in Scotland rely upon on a daily basis. 1 in 3 Scots work for a local council. 95% of Scottish children go to state schools.

Regulation. Local councils are responsible for the licensing of entertainment venues such as pubs and night clubs.

Local democracy. All local councils have elected representatives (councillors) who represent local people. It is the job of local councillors to decide how the council should spend its budget. Local councillors are often well known within the local area. They have busy jobs working within the local council and attending local meetings.

Local councillors are paid for their work. They often live in the constituency (or 'ward' in local council terms) which they represent. While councillors attend many meetings during the day, the job of a councilor is not 9–5. There are many community meetings held at night which a councilor will be often required to attend.

Dave Dempsey, is leader of the Scottish Conservative group on Fife Council. He elected as one of four councillors under the STV voting system for Ward 6, Inverkeithing, Aberdour & Dalgety Bay. Dave is a member of a number of Council committees, including Environment, Finance and Corporate Services Scrutiny Committee, South West Fife Area Committee, Standards & Audit Committee and the Superannuation Fund and Pensions Sub-Committee. Dave's interests include doing things with computers and listening to classical music as loud as possible.

"I enjoy seeing improvements in the local area. That's really what local councilors do and where we get our satisfaction; getting things done.

I support the STV system and not just because it gets me elected! At Council meetings, councilors can often be party political, but away from the Council, at meetings in the community we all work together and actually get on quite well with each other".

Like most Councillors I spend much more time on the job than we are contracted for. I go to a lot of meetings at night because there are so many active community groups in our local area. I really enjoy this aspect of the job. I don't have the traditional surgery in a community hall. Constituents can phone me or email me anytime and I pride myself in getting back to them and dealing with their issue."

Lesley Laird is a Scottish Labour councillor, elected as one of four councillors under the STV voting system for Ward 6, Inverkeithing, Aberdour & Dalgety Bay. She is a member of a number of Fife Council committees, including Environment, Finance and Corporate Services Scrutiny Committee, Social Work & Health Policy Advisory Group and South West Fife Area Committee.

"Since being elected I have found a whole new world opening up. Daily interaction with members of the public, surgeries, as well as Community Groups and Committee work the role is varied and at times challenging.

My observations of the STV system is if it is to work effectively for the electorate, it requires all ward councillors to work together, to agree areas of common ground, and then try and work towards what is best for the local community.

This can sometimes be at odds with wider political dimension – but if any one of us is to achieve anything tangible during our term in office then we have to work together."

Scottish Labour

61

THE SINGLE TRANSFERABLE VOTE IN SCOTLAND

Councillors in Scotland are elected by the proportional Single Transferable Voting System (STV). This means that most people have a number of councillors, often from different political parties, representing them. Voters have a choice of who they can go to about a local issue. Many local authorities do not have any one party in overall control and are run by coalitions of different political parties.

In STV, the voter has more than one vote. Rather than placing one "X" next to the candidate of choice, the voter will have a number of choices, ranking the candidates in order of preference I, 2, 3 etc.

So, the voter can choose not just between parties but within them. In most of Scotland's local authorities, the major political parties will field a number of candidates on the voter's ballot paper. So, a voter, if he/she wishes, could give a candidate of a party his/her number 1 vote, but give a candidate from another party his/her number 2.

In local elections where the local council candidates often live locally and will have a word of mouth reputation, STV provides an incentive for elected councillors to work hard. They cannot take the voter for granted as they may choose to vote for another candidate from the same party if he/she is not doing a good enough job.

LOCAL GOVERNMENT FUNDING

Local councils receive most of their funds from the Scottish Government. The rest of the money local councils have comes from the Council Tax, Business Rates and charges for services. The amount of Council Tax a family pays depends on the value of the family home. The more money the home is worth, the higher the monthly Council Tax will be. There are discounts for those who live alone and benefits for those on low incomes.

In difficult economic times, local councils tend to receive less money from the Scottish Government. This means that local councils have to make cuts in the vital services they provide.

WHERE LOCAL GOVERNMENT GETS ITS FUNDS

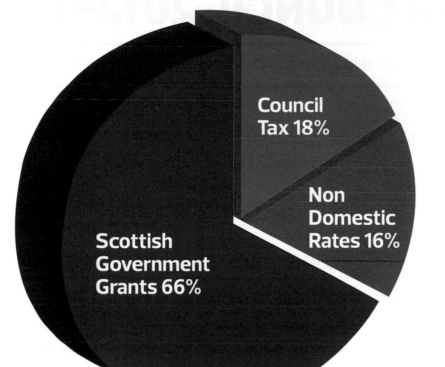

Council Tax 18%

Non Domestic Rates 16%

Scottish Government Grants 66%

HOW LOCAL GOVERNMENT SPENDS ITS FUNDS (FIFE COUNCIL 2012-13)

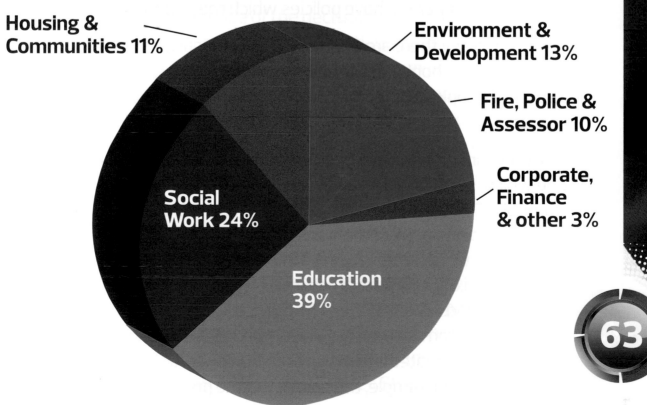

Housing & Communities 11%

Environment & Development 13%

Fire, Police & Assessor 10%

Corporate, Finance & other 3%

Social Work 24%

Education 39%

63

Pressure Group rights	Pressure Group responsibilities
To form as a group	To publish its accounts to its members explaining where how their subscriptions are spent
To set up a website and produce campaigning materials	To obey the laws of libel
To hold a demonstration	To ask police for permission to demonstrate and co-operate with the police during the march
To gather to protest outside a government building	To be peaceful and non-violent
To set up a Facebook /Twitter campaign	To not threaten or abuse people online

CASE STUDY: SP KES

SPOKES is a non-party-political campaigning group, which was established in Edinburgh in 1977. It campaigns for better conditions for cyclists, in particular in Edinburgh and the Lothians.

It aims to persuade government to encourage cycling as part of a sustainable transport and access strategy. It publicises the benefits of cycling for the community and individuals as a cheap, efficient, enjoyable, healthy, non-polluting and safe form of transport.

SPOKES lobbies the Scottish Government and local authorities for increased support for cycling as a means of transport for everyday local journeys. It puts great emphasis on encouraging its 1200 members to take action themselves, such as speaking at public meetings, writing to Government as well as maintaining cycle paths and collecting information about cycle usage. Spokes has produced several highly popular cycle maps and factsheets.

It keeps its members up to date with developments through its regular newsletters, its website, its Twitter feed (www.twitter.com/SpokesLothian) and its Facebook page (www.facebook.com/pages/Spokes-the-Lothian-Cycle-Campaign/169099526468801?fref=ts)

LEARNING ACTIVITY: PRESSURE GROUPS

Think of a social/political issue you feel strongly about. It could be human rights, cruelty to animals, vegetarianism, equality, poverty, drink driving, smoking, drugs, knife crime, sectarianism, an environmental issue ... there are many causes in which people feel something should be done. It could be a local issue within your community.

Make up a presentation on the issue. It could be on paper, on a PowerPoint or in some other format you feel confident with. Set up a Facebook page?

WITHIN YOUR PRESENTATION

Describe the key features your group believes in/what it wants to see happen

Explain your campaign methods; what you are doing to make change happen, or not happen as the case may be. Who are the decision makers you are focusing on? What can you do to put pressure on them? How can you gain publicity (in a good way!)

Make your presentation attractive. You have to convince people that your group's views are the right thing to do. Think about your language, your images, your colours, in other words, your public face. Are you scaring the public away from your cause or are you winning people over?

PARTICIPATION IN TRADE UNIONS IN SCOTLAND AND THE UK

Many working people choose to join a trade union. Trade unions are organisations which attempt to improve the pay and working conditions for their members. In return for paying a subscription, trade union members receive a wide range of benefits. These can be legal benefits such as financial help with access to a lawyer. Many trade unions offer a range of financial benefits to members such as cheaper deals with mortgages, or discounts on holidays and car purchase. Trade unions exist in a wide range of occupation and professions.

Occupation/ Profession	Trade Union/ Professional Association
Nurse/midwife /health worker	Unison: www.unison-scotland.org.uk RCN: www.rcn.org.uk/aboutus/scotland
Firefighter	FBU Scotland: www.fbuscotland.org
Teacher	EIS: www.eis.org.uk SSTA: www.ssta.org.uk/news.php
Train driver	ASLEF: www.aslef.org.uk
Bus driver	Unitescotland: www.unitescotland.org
Hotel/bar worker	GMB: www.gmb.org.uk/contact_gmb/gmb_regional_offices/gmb_scotland.aspx
Postman/woman	CWU: www.cwu.org/scotland.html
Actor	Equity: www.equity.org.uk/branches/scotland-variety-branch
Journalist	NUJ: www.nujscotland.org.uk

The trade union will negotiate with the company over money matters, such as pay and pensions. The trade union will negotiate with the company over other important matters such as holidays, hours of work and break times. The trade union will provide members with legal representation if they are disciplined at work or suffer from workplace bullying or discrimination.

Often within a workplace, a trade union representative, known as a 'shop steward' will act as a 'go-between' between worker and management. He/she will try to resolve problems which may arise.

Some employers do not recognise trade unions as they feel they are bad for business. They may feel that workers in trade unions may be more concerned about their rights at work than doing their best for the company. They may, therefore, discourage workers from joining a trade union. In very small workplaces there may be little need for workers to join a trade union as working life is informal and friendly.

Trade unions only tend to make the news when there is conflict at work, such as a strike. A strike is when trade union members vote to stop working on a particular day. The trade union members will probably lose a day's pay so trade unionists normally only go on strike when they feel very strongly about an issue. A strike is usually the last resort once all other ways of resolving the dispute have been exhausted.

Trade unions must be very careful to obey the law. For example, trade unions must hold a secret, postal ballot of their members if they wish to go on strike. If a majority of members vote to go on strike, some members of the union may still choose to go to work. By doing so, they are ignoring the democratic decision which the union members made. But going into work while the trade union is strike is perfectly legal. Trade union members can protest outside the workplace and attempt to persuade working trade union members not to go into work. This protest is called a 'picket'. By law, there can only be six trade unionists allowed to picket and they can be arrested if they try to intimidate those going into work.

Other employers understand that good worker/management relations are important. Trade unions work with workers and management on a daily basis, resolving workplace issues. Trade unions can help communication at work and solve problems which, if left to their own devices, could escalate.

Rights	Responsibilities
To join a trade union	To pay union subscriptions
To attend union meetings	To speak and respect the views of others
To vote on union issues	
	To respect the democratic wishes of the majority
To be represented by a shop steward to management	To be honest with the shop steward about any workplace difficulties

CASE STUDY: EQUITY SCOTLAND

Equity is the UK trade union for actors and performers. Set up in 1930 by a group of artists, Equity represents its members on pay and conditions like any other trade union. Equity negotiates with arts organisations over issues such as fair payments and fees for artists; health and safety regulation; royalties and members' pension and insurance schemes.

Helen Raw is the elected Secretary & Vice Chair for the East of Scotland General Branch of Equity. Helen also runs The Raw Talent Company, an actor training and film/theatre production company. Helen is currently studying full time for a double degree in Forensic Psychobiology (a Psychology and Biology degree combined with the added extra of Forensic Science). Helen has recently moved into film production and has a number of short films set for release in 2013–14.

"In summer 2008 I requested a get together of Equity members to see if there was interest in forming a branch in Scotland. I felt a wee bit isolated and wanted to proactively do something about it. With the assistance of the Regional Organisers in Glasgow, we set up an initial meeting in Edinburgh to see what the interest would be.

Over 150 people turned up and I was floored.

We then held elections and a committee was formed. The branch kicked off with its inaugural event in Jan 2009 and we have been going from strength to strength. We represent members in the East of

Scotland (and some in Glasgow) in pay and contract disputes and won our first unfair dismissal case in 2009. There are even some members down in London who call on us for help because they know me and know I will get things sorted! (not sure that's a good rep to have or not!) I am the only existing member from the first set up and have been re-elected at every Annual General Meeting since.

I am not the stereotypical trade unionist. I don't go on marches but I do put my members' issues and concerns before my own ideals and political beliefs so I think that makes me a perfect candidate for running a Union branch, albeit we are a non-party political Union.

A Facebook page has been set up for branch members and I combine the administrative elements of meetings with more engaging activities. I also co-run a Facebook group called the British Actors Network which has in excess of 1,400 members. Our Equity branch stretches from the bottom of the east coast of Scotland all the way to the Shetland Isles.

We need to make meetings of value to our members. There's no way I'd get on a train from Aberdeen to Edinburgh to attend an Equity meeting that might last twenty minutes. However, I know I'd go if there was a social or networking event going on as well. Branch meetings usually incorporate some sort of social event and have included, to date, an open mic night, a quiz night, casting director Q&A sessions at the Edinburgh International Film Festival and social drinks.''

71

INSPIRE • TRAIN • ENTERTAIN

| Home | About | Productions | Training | Education | Calendar | News | Contact | search... |

CREATE INNOVATE ENTERTAIN
FILM · THEATRE · CORPORATE EVENTS · CONSULTANCY

Raw Talent PRODUCTIONS

PRODUCTIONS

Theatre, acting and film-making are what we do best and we love it, so we incorporate our knowledge and sense of fun to create innovative team building and corporate events, produce short films and cabaret shows and direct full scale musicals.

If you are looking for go-karting, paint balling or someone to do your tax returns, we'd be rubbish!

TRAINING

If you are looking to become a better actor, you've come to the right place.

We have workshops for all levels of ability, so whether you are an established actor or a complete beginner, we have a workshop or class to suit you.

However, if you are looking to be rich & famous, please click here as it is a much quicker route and requires no skill at all.

EDUCATION & OUTREACH

Our filmmaking and drama workshops for children and young people have proven extremely popular with schools and outreach charities and encompass all 4 markers of the Curriculum for Excellence.

If you want a programme dictated by grown ups, with pre-set topics which the children and young people have no say in, you'll have to look elsewhere!

Dreams really can come true but they are most often the result of hard work, determination and persistence

Jason Blume

I set up Raw Talent because I remember how difficult and scary it was being a high school student trying to get information and advice about moving into the professional performance world. I had no idea where to go for professional training without having to move to London. Everything seemed so out of reach and elitist. How could wee lass from Rosyth and Dalgety Bay get further than the local youth theatre? No-one knew.

The Equity Card was a pipe-dream, Spotlight was the golden book I could never get into and getting an agent...don't be silly!

How great would it have been for me as that high school kid to have made a visit to one company who could have told me everything I could possibly want to know about the industry, how to move forward in my career, how to get an Equity card and an agent?

How great if that company were then available at the end of a phone or email to offer me or my parents practical advice in an honest, open and supportive environment?

How great would it have been if that company could also offer part–time, practical training and coaching that didn't break the bank but would help me build my confidence and skills, without the ridiculous promises of fame and fortune? How great if that company could potentially offer me work as an actor by producing films and creating theatre?

I'd have loved finding that company and would have felt empowered to help myself but it didn't seem to exist so...I set it up!

- **that's why most of my students come back for more.**

- **that's why many of my students move on to full time acting study.**

- **that's why 100% of my students would recommend our workshops and classes to others.**

- **that's why I get glowing references from all the non–acting clients I work with – from working with disadvantaged children on film projects for outreach charities, to writing drama resources for the Scottish Government.**

I've always thought that if you believe in yourself and don't lose sight of your roots, remain patient and courteous and stay true to your morals, you'll eventually get the long awaited break to do what you love and get paid for it. Stick in there.

www.therawtalentcompany.co.uk

LEARNING ACTIVITY: TRADE UNION ROLE PLAY

A lot of trade union work involves resolving disputes within the workplace. These can be around any number of issues. Select one of the following issues and divide your group into three. Each member of your group should play a part.

Part One: member of management

Part Two: trade union shop steward

Part Three: worker

ALCOHOL AT WORK

Scenario. Within in a call centre, a member of staff turns up for work after drinking in the pub. While the member of staff is not drunk, he/she is under the influence of alcohol which is against company policy. Management has sacked the member of staff. The trade union feels that he/she has been a good employee for some time. This is a first offence and there may be issues at home which explain this behaviour. A meeting takes place to discuss the way forward.

SEXUAL HARASSMENT AT WORK

Scenario. A large city centre office. A female member of staff approaches the trade union complaining of sexist bullying by another male member of staff, who is also a trade union member. "Jokes" are being made. The male member of staff claims the jokes are 'banter' but the female worker feels uncomfortable. She doesn't want to make herself unpopular but she now dreads coming into work and the jokes don't seem to be stopping. A meeting takes place to discuss the way forward.

WORKING HOURS CONFLICT

Scenario. A large restaurant chain. The company has good days and bad days. It is hard to tell when the restaurant will be busy. Sometimes there are bookings at short notice and staff are asked to stay on later. One of the union members has difficulty with last minute requests to work on as he is a lone parent. He has noticed that since turning down offers to work on, management is giving him more than his fair share of boring and unpleasant tasks. He feels he is being victimized and asks the union for help. A meeting takes place to discuss the way forward.

75

Chapter Three:
Skills and Knowledge

Democracy in the UK

The following information illustrates the skills and knowledge that will be assessed within the Democracy in Scotland and the United Kingdom unit of National 4 and National 5 Modern Studies. This does not mean that you will not use the other skills that Modern Studies develops. Remember also that you will be assessed in these other skills in the other two units (Social Issues in the United Kingdom and International Issues) and in the Added Value of your course.

N4: Modern Studies Skills and Knowledge

- Detecting bias and/or exaggeration using two sources of information

- Briefly explaining bias and/or exaggeration using evidence from two sources of information

- Giving straightforward descriptions of the main features of a political issue, from either Democracy in Scotland and/or the United Kingdom

- Giving straightforward explanations relating to a political issue in Scotland and/or the United Kingdom

N5: Modern Studies Skills and Knowledge

- Detecting exaggeration and/or selective use of facts using at least two and no more than four sources of information

- Explaining, in detail, exaggeration and/or selective use of facts using evidence from these sources of information

- Giving detailed descriptions of a political issue that show theoretical and factual knowledge of Democracy in Scotland and/or the United Kingdom

  - Giving detailed explanations relating to a political issue in Scotland and/or the United Kingdom

THE WORK OF AN MP

The UK public elects Members of Parliament (MPs) to represent their interests in the House of Commons.

MPs carry out duties in Parliament in Westminster and in their constituencies. Their job requires a number of different roles; working in the Parliament itself, working in the constituency that elected them and working for their political party.

MPs come from many different backgrounds; teaching, business, law and local government, although there is some concern at the increasing number of 'professional MPs'; MPs who have gone straight into politics from school and never had a 'real job'.

There are currently 650 constituencies in the UK with an average of 70,000 eligible voters in each. There are 533 in England, 59 in Scotland, 40 in Wales and 18 in Northern Ireland. An MP represents everyone in their constituency, regardless of who they voted for at the general election or even if they did not vote at all.

MP's duties at Westminster could involve:

- **assisting to make a law by speaking in debates**

- **voting to change, pass or defeat a bill**

- **working in committees**

- **scrutinising the government by asking oral or written questions**

In the House of Commons, select committees scrutinise the work of the government. Most committees focus on the work of a specific government department and all contain MPs from all the main political parties.

Prime Minister's questions takes place every Wednesday at 12 noon. This is where the Prime Minister answers questions from MPs about the work of the government. In addition, written questions can be submitted at any time.

The Prime Minister is also an MP and has responsibility for all of the work of the government. MPs who are government ministers or opposition spokespeople have responsibility for a specific policy, for example health or education.

MPs must balance parliamentary duties with constituency work. A large number of MPs hold regular surgeries at their office or local town halls. Local constituents can come along to discuss any matters that concern them. Constituents can also arrange to meet their MP at Parliament.

MPs can attend meetings and give speeches on particular topics. It is also important that they attend functions, visit schools, businesses and generally try to meet as many people as possible. This gives MPs further insight and knowledge into issues and topics they may discuss when they return to Westminister.

Jo Swinson MP

Born: 5 February 1980

Educated: Douglas Academy, Milngavie, London school of Economics.

Party: Liberal Democrat

Represents: Glasgow

Interests: Quality of life and wellbeing, climate change, allergy, foreign affairs, corporate social responsibility.

Countries of Interest: Chechnya, India, Kosovo, Romania, Sierra Leone

In September 2012, Jo Swinson became Minister for Employment Relations, Consumer and Postal Affairs in the Department for Business, Innovation and Skills and Equalities Minister in the Department of Culture, Media and Sport.)

79

A TYPICAL DIARY OF AN MP WOULD BE...

MONDAY

- Westminster – Meet with staff
- Speaking in key debate in the House of Commons chamber
- Committee meeting– London Olympics Bill Committee
- Committee meeting– final amendments before bill is passed

TUESDAY

- Westminster – Meeting regarding Body Confidence Campaign
- Speaking at a debate regarding Business, Innovation and Skills, specifically on the Living Wage.
- Government meeting
- Speaking at Body Image Debate

WEDNESDAY

- Westminster – Meeting a school group from constituency who are visiting the Parliament
- Meeting with national charity
- Government meeting

Most MPs have their own website. Many MPs are now using social media to inform constituents of their work

THURSDAY

- Westminster – Meeting with Public Bill Committee: Groceries Code Adjudicator
- Brief for Prime Ministers Questions
- Prime Ministers Questions
- Travel to Glasgow in the evening.

FRIDAY

- Constituency Day – Meet with staff
- School visit
- Council meeting on specific topic concerning constituents
- Meeting with local business to discuss job cuts
- Surgery in local town hall

SATURDAY

- Surgery in constituency office
- Lunch at pensioners group
- Door knocking in one area of constituency
- Speech at local charity dinner

SUNDAY

- Appearance at local sports club
- Meeting voluntary youth group
- Door knocking in another area of the constituency
- Travel to London

LEARNING ACTIVITY: THE WORK OF AN MP

Imagine you are the MP for your constituency:

www.parliament.uk/mps-lords-and-offices

You can be a member of any political party you choose.

Design a Twitter feed for your typical week.

Think of issues that have been going on in your constituency and in Parliament.

PASSING LEGISLATION

Our laws of the land first appear as a Parliamentary Bill. To become law the text of a Bill must be agreed by both Houses. Either House can vote down a Bill in which case it will normally not become law – but there are exceptions. The Commons can pass the same Bill in two successive years, in which case it can become law without the agreement of the Lords. Bills which are only about money (raising taxes or authorising government expenditure) are not opposed in the Lords and may only be delayed for a month.

Both Houses of Parliament hold debates in which Members discuss government policy, proposed new laws and current issues.

Debates are designed to assist MPs and Lords to reach an informed decision on a subject. Votes are often held to conclude a debate, which may involve then passing or rejecting a proposed new law (legislation) or simply registering their opinion on a subject. All debates are recorded in a publication called 'Hansard' which is available online or in print.

DEBATING IN THE COMMONS

Commons debates are often lively, with MPs often interrupting each other. One of the roles of The Speaker of the House of Commons is to keep order and allow debates to be heard. "Unparliamentary" language is not allowed. For example, MPs are not allowed to call another MP a "liar".

The House of Commons has a number of bizarre traditions. One is "Dragging the Speaker". When a new Speaker of the House of Commons is elected, the successful candidate is physically dragged to the Chair by other MPs.

This custom dates back to when it was the Speaker's role to explain the Commons' view to the monarch. If the monarch didn't like the Commons' view, there was the possibility he may be killed. Hence why, in the past, there was reluctance by some MPs to become The Speaker.

Debates are an opportunity for MPs to voice the concerns and interests of their constituents. To participate in a debate in the House of Commons or at Question Time, MPs have to be called by the Speaker. MPs usually rise or half-rise from their seats in a bid to get the Speaker's attention – this is known as 'catching the Speaker's eye'.

In reality, all the major parties have MPs known as 'whips' whose job is to make sure that MPs put their loyalty to their party before their constituents or anyone else. In the modern era most MPs are elected because they are representatives of a political party. It is extremely difficult for someone to be elected to Parliament as an 'independent'. The party whips remind MPs of this. Failure to support the party will mean 'the whip being withdrawn'. This will result in the MP being banned from party meetings and unlikely to be considered for promotion. He/she may well be dropped as the party's candidate at the next General Election.

The Government needs to retain the confidence of a majority in the House of Commons. If Opposition parties call for a 'vote of no confidence' in the Government and the Government loses the vote, the Government must call a General Election. The last time this happened was 1979.

The House of Lords is a flawed, undemocratic institution

Nick Clegg

in government on your side

REFORM OF THE HOUSE OF LORDS

As noted earlier, the House of Lords has important powers in passing legislation. It can delay and amend bills passed by the House of Commons Yet none of its members are elected.

The UK is alone among leading democratic nations in having people run the country who are completely unaccountable to the people.

MPs of all parties have been seeking to reform the House of Lords for a long time. But all attempts to elect members to the House of Lords have failed. Liberal Democrat leader Nick Clegg is just the latest to try. In August 2012, his bid failed when Labour and Conservative MPs blocked his plans.

Nick Clegg wanted 4/5 of members of the Lords to be elected. The number of peers would have been almost halved, from 826 to 450. They would have served 15–year terms of office, after which they could stand for re–election.

Peers would have represented a specific part of the United Kingdom, elected via the Single Transferable Vote system of proportional representation.

Some peers would continue to be appointed by the Prime Minister although the number of Church of England bishops would have been reduced. All hereditary peers would have been removed.

Some Labour MPs wanted the Lords to be completely elected. Some Conservative MPs argued that with the country in economic difficulty the Government should have other priorities. The Coalition Government abandoned the House of Lords Reform Bill in August 2012 after around 100 Conservative MPs vowed to vote with Labour in opposing it.

For an elected Lords	Against an elected Lords
The Lords is a relic of a by–gone age. All people who represent the people should be elected.	The Lords, like the Royal Family is a British Institution. Its members are experienced and represent the wisdom of generations.
Appointment to the Lords is a 'jobs for the boys' exercise, where the Prime Minister gives out jobs to his friends and supporters.	Being unelected has its advantages. Peers in the Lords are not political party minded the way MPs are. They look at bills on their merits rather whether or not they will get them elected again.
Most peers in the Lords are wealthy people with little idea of the lives of ordinary voters.	Many peers are appointed because they have real skills and expertise. By contrast, many MPs these days have never had 'real jobs' having only worked in politics.

LEARNING ACTIVITY: REFORM OF THE HOUSE OF LORDS AND DEVELOPING AN ARGUMENT

Divide into four groups, each one with a large piece of paper.

Two groups should support reform of the House of Lords and two should oppose it.

Each group should write down all the ideas that come to mind for their position. By the end of the activity, they should decide the top two reasons why their viewpoint is correct.

Each group should present their reasons and answer any questions from the opposing groups, justifying, in detail, if possible, why their viewpoint is correct.

VOTING AND THE FIRST PAST THE POST VOTING SYSTEM

If you are aged 18 or over you can vote in General Elections in the UK. In order to be eligible to vote, you must be registered with your local electoral office.

There are a number of ways in which you can vote. Most people vote in person at a polling station on election day. You are given a ballot paper listing the candidates standing for election and the parties they represent. You vote by putting a cross by the name of person you want to be MP. The ballot paper is then folded in half and put in a locked ballot box. Individuals can also vote by post. You must apply in advance through your local electoral registration office.

The voting system used in the UK Parliament is First Past the Post (FPTP). It is called this as the party which gets "first past the post" of half the number of constituency seats in the House of Commons can normally form a Government. There are 650 parliamentary constituencies in the UK. To win a constituency (usually referred to as a 'seat'), a candidate only needs one more vote than their nearest rival. A party, therefore, which can win more than 325 seats, will normally form the Government.

MARGINAL SEAT 2010: HAMPSTEAD & KILBURN (LONDON)

Candidate	Party	Number of votes	Percentage of votes	Majority
Glenda Jackson	Labour	17,332	32.8	42
Chris Philp	Conservative	17,290	32.7	
Edward Fordham	Liberal Democrat	16,491	31.2	
Bea Campbell	Green	759	1.4	
Magnus Nielsen	UK Independence Party	408	0.8	
Victoria Moore	British National Party	328	0.6	
Tamsin Omond	Tamsin Omond To The Commons	123	0.2	
Gene Alcantara	Independent	91	0.2	

The Electoral Reform Society estimated that 382 out of the 650 seats contested in the General Election were 'Super Safe'. 172 of these were Conservative, 165 were Labour, 29 were Liberal Democrat, 3 were SNP and 2 were Plaid Cymru. 11 out of the 18 UK Parliament seats in Northern Ireland were Super Safe, reflecting the entrenched voting patterns of Northern Irish politics.

What this means is that, in reality, for UK elections, we have two classes of voter; those who vote in safe seats and those who vote in marginal seats. In safe seats, the voters can more or less be ignored by the political parties. The 'winners' know they will win, so do not spend time and money listening to the views of voters who live there. The 'losers' will run only a token campaign, often fielding a young inexperienced candidate or anyone really who can be bothered!

After the election, there is little incentive, other than personal pride for the MP to work hard for his/her constituents. Instead, it more important that the MP pleases his/her party in order to be re-selected for a safe seat, the election for which is almost a foregone conclusion.

By contrast, the 'real' election is fought in the marginal seats. These are the seats where every vote counts. Voters who live in these seats know this. They know the candidates from all parties have to listen to them. The political parties will spend a lot of time and money wooing voters. In addition, the MP who eventually wins this seat must keep his/her constituents content while he/she is in Parliament. They will have elected an MP who will work hard to represent them.

So, do we have some voters who are more listened to and better represented than others?

First Past the Post Advantages	First Past the Post Disadvantages
FPTP allows the most popular candidate to win the election. This is fair as the most popular wins. FPTP has one vote for one candidate. This is fair as it forces the voter to think and vote for the candidate they think is the best. FPTP means that voters know who their elected representative will be and who the representative till the next election is. It is fair because it means the voter will know who to contact and be able to form an opinion on him/her before the next election.	FPTP is not proportional. This is unfair in modern party politics as most voters vote for parties not individuals. A party that gets a high percentage of the vote can receive a low percentage of the representation. In FPTP there are many "safe" seats where most voters know who will win before the campaign starts. This is unfair as those who vote for opposition parties have no incentive to vote at all as their vote will be wasted. In FPTP, parties focus their attentions on voters in "marginal seats". This is unfair as voters in these seats get more attention than those in "safe" seats.

A PROPORTIONAL SYSTEM?

One alternative to the FPTP voting system is the Single Transferable Voting system used for elections to Scottish local councils.

Here, there are larger constituencies (called 'wards' in Scottish local councils). Instead of placing one 'X' next to the one candidate of choice, voters can rank candidates 1, 2, 3, 4 etc.

In STV, it is more complicated working out who gets elected. But this is done by computer software. In deciding who gets elected, the number of first preference votes a candidate receives is calculated. Candidates who reach a certain 'quota' of votes, based on the voting population and how many candidates, are elected.

Overall, STV tends to provide a more proportional result. Unlike FPTP, voters don't have to 'put all their eggs in one basket'. They may like more than one candidate and can reflect this in how they vote. Parties also can stand more than one candidate if they wish.

Depending on the voting population of the ward, voters will have a number of representatives.

Here is an example from the Inverkeithing and Dalgety Bay ward in Fife, where four candidates are elected.

FIFE COUNCIL ELECTION 2012 INVERKEITHING AND DALGETY BAY WARD

Candidate	Party	First Preference Votes received
Mike Arthur	UKIP	182
Dave Dempsey *	Con	832
Lesley Laird *	Lab	960
Alice McGarry *	SNP	1377
Helen Todd	SNP	662
Dave Walker	Lib Dem	497
Gavin Yates *	Lab	877

*Elected candidates

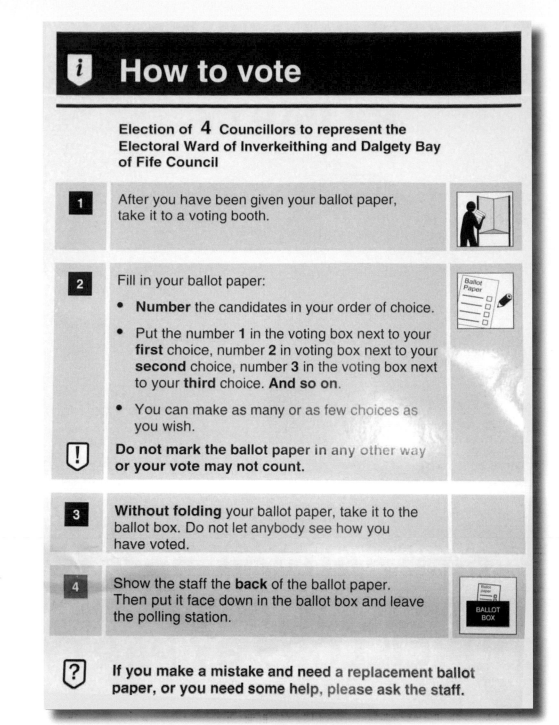

How to vote

Election of **4** Councillors to represent the Electoral Ward of Inverkeithing and Dalgety Bay of Fife Council

1 After you have been given your ballot paper, take it to a voting booth.

2 Fill in your ballot paper:

- **Number** the candidates in your order of choice.

- Put the number **1** in the voting box next to your **first** choice, number **2** in voting box next to your **second** choice, number **3** in the voting box next to your **third** choice. **And so on**.

- You can make as many or as few choices as you wish.

Do not mark the ballot paper in any other way **or your vote may not count.**

3 **Without folding** your ballot paper, take it to the ballot box. Do not let anybody see how you have voted.

4 Show the staff the **back** of the ballot paper. Then put it face down in the ballot box and leave the polling station.

? **If you make a mistake and need** a replacement ballot **paper, or you need some help,** please ask the staff.

FIFE COUNCIL 2012 PARTY REPRESENTATION

Scottish Labour	35
Scottish National Party	26
Scottish Liberal Democrat	10
Scottish Conservative	3
Other	1
Total number of Councillors	**75**

FIFE COUNCIL 2012 PERCENTAGE OF VOTES BY PARTY

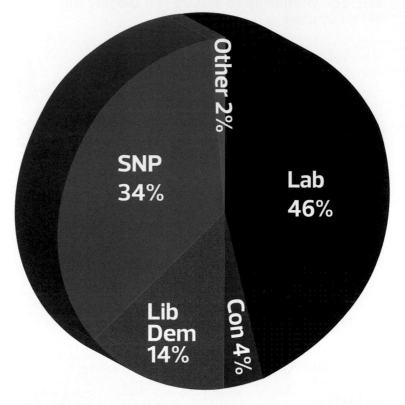

Other 2%

SNP
34%

Lab
46%

Lib
Dem
14%

Con 4%

FIFE COUNCIL 2012 PERCENTAGE OF COUNCILLORS BY PARTY

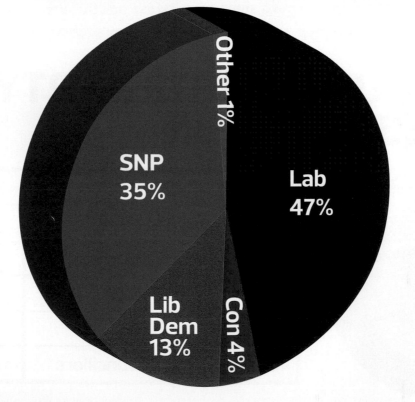

Other 1%

SNP
35%

Lab
47%

Lib
Dem
13%

Con 4%

STV Advantages	STV Disadvantages
Voters can vote for more than one candidate	Voters have more than one representative, could be confused who to speak to
Overall result tends to be more proportional	Voters could be confused as to who is actually in charge
There are no safe seats, every vote counts	Voters could be confused who to vote for

LEARNING ACTIVITY: EXTENDED WRITING ON VOTING SYSTEMS

- **Decide whether you think FPTP should be replaced by a proportional voting system, such as the Single Transferable Vote**

- **Explain your argument in detail, if possible, using evidence and examples**

- **Justify why you think the your voting system is the fairest**

- **Write your arguments in the form of a letter to a newspaper**

THE MEDIA AND THE 2010 GENERAL ELECTION

The media plays a powerful role in our democracy. It is no surprise that countries which do not have a democratic system, such as China, have a Government which strictly controls what we read, see and hear.

The UK has always been proud of its traditions of freedom of speech, freedom to express a point of point of view and the freedom to publish points of view be it in newspapers, books, magazines, radio and increasingly these days, online.

With these rights come responsibilities. The laws of slander mean that a person or organization can be taken in court for making harmful or untrue statements about someone else/another organisation. The laws of libel mean a person or organization can be taken to court for publishing harmful or untrue statements about someone else/another organization. The laws of libel apply to online communication; websites, blogs and social media too not just the print media. There are many examples of people/organisations being successfully sued for making inaccurate or damaging accusations.

By law, television organisations must provide balanced and unbiased coverage of political events. They are not supposed to favour any one political party or point of view. News programmes, for example on BBC or the commercial channels must hold the Government to account by asking challenging questions. They must have spokespersons from different points of view.

By contrast, the print media; be it newspapers or online, can be as biased as it likes. Newspapers are free to support any political party, cause or viewpoint. British newspapers have traditions of supporting a political party. Indeed some people may choose to buy a newspaper because of its overall political approach.

There are differences between 'quality' newspapers and tabloids. Examples of 'quality' newspapers are The Guardian, The Independent, The Times, The Daily Telegraph, or here in Scotland, The Herald and The Scotsman. These newspapers contain a lot of political news. They cover news stories, at home and abroad, in detail. They usually attempt to be unbiased and cover differing points of view. They normally support a political party or certain social/moral viewpoints. But they show this in a special section called 'The Editorial', which is a column where it explains what it thinks about a particular issue.

On the other hand, the tabloids (or 'red tops') are much more aggressive and biased in their reporting of political issues. Examples of tabloids are The Sun, The Daily Express, The Daily Mail and, in Scotland, the Scottish version of The Sun and The Daily Record. Tabloids often campaign against a particular issue, devoting big headlines attacking the Government or individuals. While they devote a lot of space to stories about celebrities and sport, they are also highly political. Their stories are often emotive, focusing on real life human experiences rather than the political process. At election time tabloid newspapers are frequently very biased in favour or against a political party.

They can show their support in a number of ways. They can include good news stories about the party they support. They can publish bad news stories about the parties they do not support. They can show flattering photographs of the leader they support. They can publish unflattering images of the leaders they do not like. They can run sustained campaigns of 'propaganda' where they 'drip drip' good news about the party support and bad news about the parties they do not. In the run up to election day itself, many pages can be devoted to biased coverage, including 'pull out' sections packed with images and loaded political messages.

The media world is changing. There are numerous TV channels with multiple news programmes on 24/7. Sales of national newspapers have been in decline for a number of years. Many working people find it difficult to find the time to read, especially read quality newspapers. 'Free' newspapers such The Metro, with its 'chunks' of news offer an alternative to commuters to buying a daily newspaper. Many people can now get their news online for free. Twitter, especially, carries news instantly and allows people to comment and/or communicate with newsmakers directly.

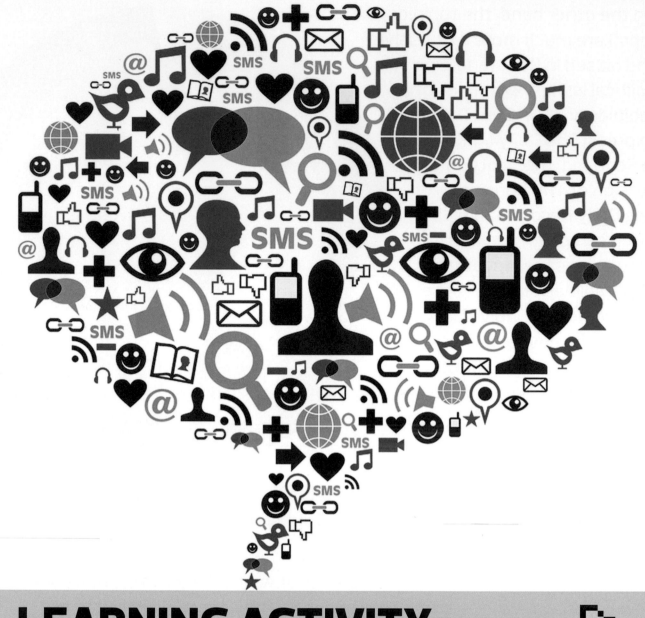

LEARNING ACTIVITY: NEWSPAPERS/ DIGITAL MEDIA

Create your own newspaper front/blog post on the 2010 General Election outcome.

Decide which political party you support and 'spin' the information to make the outcome as positive as possible for your favourite.

Provide your account of how the 2010 General Election went.

Without telling any lies or making up stories, it should contain the best possible news for your favourite, describing and explaining the most encouraging aspects of the campaign and the results.

THE 2010 GENERAL ELECTION

The 2010 General Election was the closest in a generation. For the first time since 1974, no one party won an overall majority of MPs. The Conservative Party, led by David Cameron, won the most seats and agreed to form a 'coalition government' with the Liberal Democrats who won the third largest amount of seats. Liberal leader Nick Clegg was appointed Deputy Prime Minister by new Prime Minister David Cameron. Cabinet posts were shared between Conservative and Liberal Democrat MPs.

The Green Party gained its first MP, Caroline Lucas, who was elected to represent the constituency of Brighton Pavilion.

THE LEADERS DEBATES

The 2010 General Election was the first to feature direct, head–to–head televised debates between the leaders of the three largest UK parties (The SNP's leader, Alex Salmond was not invited as, in UK terms, the SNP is not a large party). These debates captured the attention of the public and attracted large televised audiences. Around 10 million people watched the first debate on ITV.

Liberal Democrat leader Nick Clegg performed very well and the rise in support for the Liberal Democrats in the polls led many to believe the leaders' debates would have a decisive influence. But, the Liberal Democrats' share of the vote went up just 1% from the 2005 General Election.

LEARNING ACTIVITY: EXAGGERATION AND SELECTIVITY IN USE OF FACTS

Study the following sources and answer the questions. Use the evidence contained in the sources.

SOURCE 1 OPINION POLL ON THE LEADERS' DEBATE

Who do you think performed best in last night's televised leaders' debate?

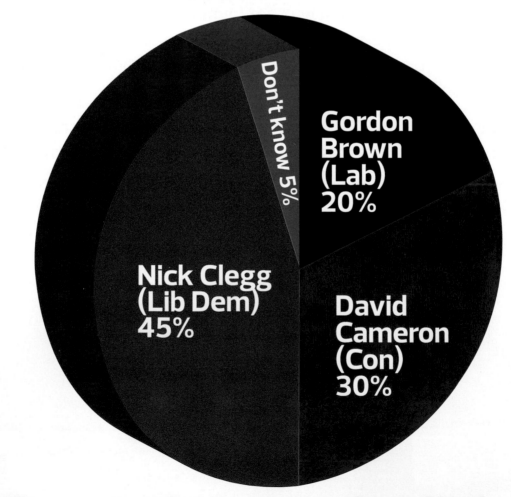

Don't know 5%

Gordon Brown (Lab) 20%

Nick Clegg (Lib Dem) 45%

David Cameron (Con) 30%

"Everybody agrees that Nick Clegg was the best performer in the leaders' debate" **View of Tony Newman**

What evidence is there that Tony Newman is exaggerating?

SOURCE 2: SEATS WON BY PARTY

2010 ■   2005 ■

	Con	Lab	Lib Dem	SNP

(Y-axis: 0, 50, 100, 150, 200, 250, 300, 350, 400)

SOURCE 3: PERCENTAGE OF VOTES WON BY PARTY

SNP 2%

Others 10%

Con 36%

Lib Dem 23%

Lab 29%

SOURCE 4: ENGLAND AND SCOTLAND COMPARED

Party	Number of votes won in England	Percentage of votes won in England	Number of votes won in Scotland	Percentage of votes won in Scorland
Con	9,908,169	39.6	412,855	16.7
Lab	7,042,398	28.1	1,035,528	42.0
Lib Dem	6,076,189	24.2	465,471	18.9
SNP			491,386	19.9

"The 2010 election result was very bad for Labour. The party lost more seats than any other did since the last general election in 2005. By contrast, the Conservatives were by far the most popular party, winning a clear majority of the votes. There is little difference in the parties people in Scotland and England vote for." **View of Kirsty Reid**

Using sources 2, 3 and 4, explain in detail, if you can, the extent to which Kirsty Reid could be accused of being selective in the use of facts.

THE PRESS

Of the daily newspapers available in Scotland, only The Daily Mirror and The Daily Record backed Labour. On election day, The Daily Mirror published a list of constituencies where the Conservatives could be beaten through 'tactical voting' by Labour and Liberal Democrat voters. It published a list of constituencies where Labour voters should vote Liberal Democrat in order to beat the Conservative candidate and others where Liberal Democrat voters should vote Labour in order to defeat the Conservative candidate.

The Sun, The Times, The Daily Telegraph, The Daily Mail and The Daily Express all backed the Conservatives. The Sun had, since 1997, urged its readers to vote Labour. But in in 2010 it switched sides to the Conservatives. It traditionally boasts of always backing the winner. But it usually waits to see who is most likely to win before it decides who to support.

The Guardian switched its support from Labour to the Liberal Democrats.

103

PARTY POLICIES

At modern General Elections, the major political parties like to highlight the personal qualities of their leader, emphasising his/her qualities to be a good Prime Minister.

The parties publish their policies in a 'manifesto'. This is their 'contract' with the voters should they be elected to form a Government. Few voters actually read the manifesto though. Most will form their opinion of the party from what they see in the media; either through the TV news or newspapers. Sometimes voters will watch a party election broadcast. Increasingly the parties are using the new media of Facebook and Twitter to get across their 'big idea'. The big idea is each party's vision of what it wants to do should it be elected. It is the one idea it wants voters to remember.

CONSERVATIVE PARTY: LEADER DAVID CAMERON

BIG IDEA: FIX "THE BROKEN SOCIETY" BY BUILDING A "BIG SOCIETY".

The Conservative Party campaigned on the idea that Britain is "broken" by poverty, unemployment and crime.

The country can only be "healed" by the public taking greater responsibility over their own lives and the wider community.

So, policies included;

encouraging parents and charities to set up new academy schools,

giving people the power to veto council tax rises through local referendums,

promising communities the right to buy their local pub or post office

The Conservatives promised

to reverse the government's proposed National Insurance rise

to raise the inheritance tax threshold to £1m

to freeze council tax for two years

to increase NHS spending in real terms every year

LABOUR PARTY: LEADER GORDON BROWN

BIG IDEA: ONLY LABOUR CAN BE TRUSTED TO LOOK AFTER THE VULNERABLE.

Labour's "big idea" was that the party saved the economy after the banks collapsed in 2008. Therefore, only Labour could be trusted to protect the vulnerable when the Government has to pay back the money the country owes (the budget deficit). It argued that the Conservatives would favour the wealthy.

Labour promised not to raise income tax rates.

Other plans are to tackle under-performing schools, hospitals and police forces by having them taken over by teams from more successful organisations.

Labour promised a "toddler tax credit" which would provide £4 per week extra for families with one and two-year-olds from 2012.

Cancer test results would be available within a week.

The National Minimum Wage would rise in line with average earnings by the end of the next Parliament.

LIBERAL DEMOCRAT: LEADER NICK CLEGG

BIG IDEA: FAIRNESS.

The Liberal Democrats' "big idea" was fairness. It claimed it was the only party who would be fair in the economic and political changes Britain requires.

The Liberal Democrats would scrap income tax on earnings up to £10,000.

They also promised to protect the state pension and increase pay for service personnel.

There would be no tuition fees for UK students at English universities

ID cards would be scrapped and the Trident nuclear programme would not be renewed.

As part of their "clean up" of UK politics, the party would limit political donations to £10,000, give people the power to sack errant MPs and introduce the single transferable vote system (STV).

SCOTTISH NATIONAL PARTY: LEADER ALEX SALMOND

BIG IDEA: ELECT SCOTTISH 'CHAMPIONS'.

The SNP does not stand in elections outside of Scotland. It cannot, therefore win a UK General Election. So, its "big idea" was the concept of electing 'local SNP champions' across Scotland in order to 'protect' Scotland from the cuts in public services which it argued would be brought in by a UK Government..

It campaigned on:

not renewing the Trident nuclear fleet

abolishing the Scottish Office

building a new River Forth crossing

increasing payments for Scottish war veterans

LEARNING ACTIVITY: MOCK ELECTION

Adopt one of the major political parties (or a smaller one such as UKIP or the Green Party)

You will be able to find their most up to date policies on the respective party websites

www.conservatives.com

www.greenparty.org.uk

www.labour.org.uk

www.libdems.org.uk/home.aspx

www.snp.org

www.ukip.org

You could make

- **Posters**

- **Leaflets**

- **Badges**

- **An election broadcast**

- **A blog page**

- **A website home page**

You should divide up the jobs between members of your group, giving everyone something meaningful to do.

In all your communications you should include

Your party branding; party logo, making sure your colours are coordinated in your party's colours.

Your big idea which you want to get across to the voters. You can also have 'negative' messages about the other parties (but not negative messages about your fellow learners in those groups!)

PRESSURE GROUPS IN THE UK

Pressure groups are organisations which try to influence government. Pressure groups do not wish to be the Government, although sometimes representatives of pressure groups stand for election, they just seek to influence government to have policies which they approve of.

In any democracy there are a wide range of pressure groups for just about any interest, cause or hobby. Trade unions are pressure groups that represent the interests of people at work. We look at trade unions in more detail on pages 68–75.

Some pressure groups have been around for a very long time. Their cause is one which is unlikely to go away any time soon. For example, the Royal Automobile Club (RAC) was formed in 1897 and has over 7 million members. While many join to protect themselves against car breakdown, the RAC has its own group which represents the interests of road users (www.racfoundation.org). It puts pressure on the government to build roads, maintain roads and, in general, improve the lives of motorists.

Often a pressure group, such as the RAC, will have other groups who believe in the same cause who act as rivals in recruiting members in order to make their organisation more powerful. The RAC has many competitor organisations. But, as a pressure group, like many other pressure groups, it will have counter-pressure groups, groups which believe in entirely the opposite. Countering the RAC will be any number of anti-car, environmentalist groups, perhaps the oldest and most famous being Greenpeace (www.greenpeace.org.uk). A more recent addition to the anti-car lobby is The Campaign for Better Transport (www.bettertransport.org.uk).

Some pressure groups have good relations with government. These will often be groups who have specialist knowledge of an issue and who

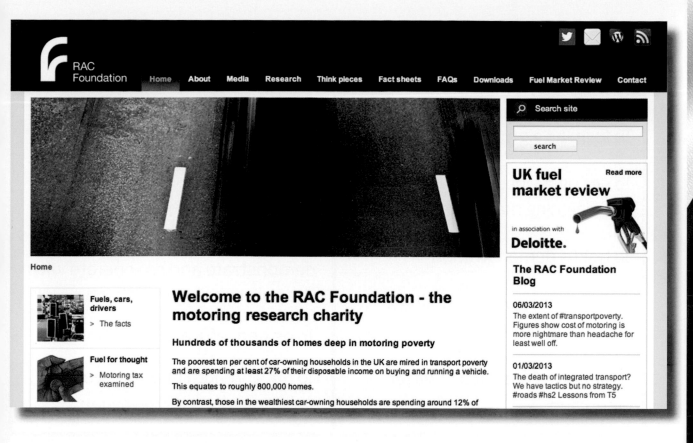

pursue goals which government approves of. Rather than the pressure group approaching Government, Government will approach the pressure group for advice and comment. These groups are usually referred to as 'insider groups' because they are inside the decision making process. The Institute of Directors (www.iod.com) is one such insider group. The Institute of Directors is a business pressure group. Government is always keen to listen to the views of business.

On the other hand, there are a wide range of pressure groups whose aims are not necessarily always shared by government. These groups are referred to as 'outsider' groups as they are outside of the decision making process. A good example of an outsider group is the Stop The War Coalition (www.stopwar.org.uk). It campaigns against much of the British Government's foreign policy. It is highly unlikely that the Stop The War Coalition will be invited by the Government for advice and guidance on foreign policy!

Pressure groups that are focused and have public support can be successful. The Gurkha Justice Campaign (www.gurkhajustice.org.uk) was a classic example of effective pressure group campaigning. The Nepalese Gurkhas have fought on Britain's side in many conflicts for over 200 years. Yet, the then Labour Government refused to let retired Gurkha servicemen live in the UK. The campaign, led by actress Joanna Lumley, whose father served with the 6th Gurkha Rifles, won all retired Gurkhas the right to live in the UK.

Pressure Group rights	Pressure Group responsibilities
To form as a group	To publish its accounts to its members explaining where how their subscriptions are spent
To set up a website and produce campaigning materials	To obey the laws of libel
To hold a demonstration	To ask police for permission to demonstrate and co-operate with the police during the march
To gather to protest outside a government building	To be peaceful and non-violent
To set up a Facebook/Twitter campaign	To not threaten or abuse people online

CASE STUDY: THE HILLSBOROUGH JUSTICE CAMPAIGN

www.facebook.com/HJCOfficial

In April 1989, 96 Liverpool football fans died after they were crushed within Sheffield Wednesday's Hillsborough stadium during the 1989 FA Cup semi-final with Nottingham Forest.

At the time, the fans' behaviour was blamed for the tragedy. It was alleged that the fans were drunk and wouldn't listen to police advice. The Sun newspaper, infamously, reported that some Liverpool fans picked the pockets of dead fans lying on the pitch.

The Hillsborough Justice Campaign was formed in 1998 to achieve 'justice' for the fans who died. It claimed that it was mistakes by the South Yorkshire police and Sheffield Wednesday stewards which led to the tragedy. It also claimed that the police lied and covered up the truth about what really went on. The Hillsborough Justice Campaign wanted to clear the name of the Liverpool supporters and to hold any police officers who lied to account.

The Hillsborough Justice Campaign put pressure on Government to hold an independent inquiry into what happened at the Hillsborough stadium.

It gave out over 100,000 leaflets at football matches across the UK and abroad.

It asked its supporters to write to MPs asking for an inquiry.

It asked its supporters to raise awareness by phoning radio talk shows and writing to newspapers.

A Facebook page was set up. Many organisations, including pop stars and footballers made financial donations to enable the group to keep up its campaigns.

Eventually, in February 2010, the Hillsborough Independent Panel was set up. It reported in September 2012. It concluded that "The evidence shows conclusively that Liverpool fans neither caused nor contributed to the deaths of 96 men, women and children". Prime Minister David Cameron told the Commons that police covered up their role and carried out a campaign to smear the dead.

LEARNING ACTIVITY: PRESSURE GROUPS

Think of a social/political issue you feel strongly about. It could be human rights, cruelty to animals, vegetarianism, equality, poverty, drink driving, smoking, drugs, knife crime, sectarianism, an environmental issue ... there are many causes in which people feel something should be done. It could be a local issue within your community.

Make up a presentation on the issue. It could be on paper, on a PowerPoint or in some other format you feel confident with. Set up a Facebook page?

WITHIN YOUR PRESENTATION

Describe the key features your group believes in/what it wants to see happen.

Explain your campaign methods; what you are doing to make change happen, or not happen as the case may be. Who are the decision makers you are focusing on? What can you do to put pressure on them? How can you gain publicity (in a good way!)

Make your presentation attractive. You have to convince people that your group's views are the right thing to do. Think about your language, your images, your colours, in other words, your public face. Are you scaring the public away from your cause or are you winning people over?

Chapter Four:
Applying Skills and Knowledge
ASSESSMENT

This chapter of the textbook deals with the ways in which you can get the best possible result in your Modern Studies course, either at National 4 or at National 5.

The content of the textbook has been designed to challenge both National 4 and National 5 learners. However, the assessment for National 4 and National 5 is quite different.

NATIONAL 4 ASSESSMENT

Like the other social studies qualifications, National 4 Modern Studies is internally assessed by your teacher within the school/college. This internal assessment is checked by SQA.

To gain the award you are required to pass the internal assessments for:

- National 4 Democracy in Scotland and the UK unit

- National 4 Social Issues in the United Kingdom unit

- National 4 International Issues unit

- National 4 The Added Value unit: The Modern Studies Assignment

115

NATIONAL 5 ASSESSMENT

Like the other social studies qualifications, National 5 Modern Studies contains both internal assessment by your teacher within the school/college (checked by the SQA) and external assessment by the SQA.

To gain the award you are required to pass the internal assessments for:

- National 5 Democracy in Scotland and the UK unit

- National 5 Social Issues in the United Kingdom unit

- National 5 International Issues unit

So, in terms of reading this chapter, please read the general advice and suggestions for Modern Studies Assignment Topics or Issues and Sources of Information. Then, if you have agreed with your teacher that you will be presented for National 4 Modern Studies, your focus will be on the advice and suggestions for National 4 Assessment (pages 126–131). Likewise, if you have agreed with your teacher that you will be presented for National 5 Modern Studies, your focus will be on the advice and suggestions for National 5 Assessment (pages 132–151).

MODERN STUDIES ASSIGNMENT TOPICS OR ISSUES

The Modern Studies Assignment is a new method of assessment in Modern Studies. It builds on the skills you have developed in earlier years in school. More specifically, it allows you the opportunity to take ownership of an issue in Modern Studies that interests you. The Modern Studies Assignment therefore hands you the opportunity to do really well. This chapter explains what you need to do and suggests some possible topics or issues you may wish to base your Modern Studies Assignment on.

These topics or issues are all within the Democracy in Scotland and the United Kingdom unit. You do not need to select a topic from this unit, you can choose a topic or issue from one of the other two Modern Studies units: Social Issues in the United Kingdom or International Issues. Advice and suggestions for the Modern Studies Assignment in these units are contained in our National 4/National 5 Social Issues in the United Kingdom and International Issues textbooks.

It should be emphasised that, while you have the choice and opportunity, it would be wise to discuss your choice with your Modern Studies teacher. He or she will be able to offer you expert guidance on how best to approach the topic or issue and will know the best and most accessible sources of information. No-one produces the perfect Modern Studies Assignment on their own. Your dialogue with your teacher is critical and asking for help is a sign of strength, not weakness. The skill of thinking through ideas, using sources of information, taking advice, and re-drafting your work, is a skill you will draw upon many times in your life at work and in further/higher education.

These potential Modern Studies Assignment topics or issues can be studied at either National 4 or National 5. They are just some of the topics or issues you could study within the Social Issues in the United Kingdom unit. The topics and issues are only suggestions, based on the topics and issues contained within this textbook. There are many more.

You may well wish to provide a local dimension to what you study. You may well find that a focus on the issue from a local or (as well as) a national dimension may improve your Assignment. You may find it easier to get information locally and your Modern Studies Assignment will stand out from the more 'off the peg' topics.

Topic/Issue	Possible focus
Voting systems	Is AMS/FPTP/STV fair?
Political Parties	Conservative/ Greens/Labour/ /Liberal Democrats/Scottish National Party/Scottish Socialist Party. Why do people vote for this party?
Pressure Groups: Choose one	What are their aims and methods?
Daily newspaper: Choose one	How does it try and influence politics?
Scottish Parliament	Should it have more powers?
House of Lords	Should it be elected?
The Prime Minister	Is he/she too powerful?
The First Minister	Is he/she too powerful?
My local council	Does it provide value for money?
Trade union: Choose one	How does it represent its members?
Digital media	Is it replacing the "old media"?
Scotland's future	Is independence the answer?
The European Union	Should the UK leave?
My local MP/MSP/Councillor	Does he/she represent his/her constituents well?
Pressure Group: Choose one	How successful has it been?

SOURCES OF INFORMATION

There is a massive range of sources of information. In the modern world, the challenge is not having enough information it's in processing that information; knowing which information you can trust to be reliable, selecting the most relevant information for your needs and communicating that information clearly to your audience.

The wrong thing to do, of course, is to go to any old website, or even an online library such as Wikipedia, copy what's there without thinking about it and pass this information off as your own. Even if you thought this is a good idea, your teacher would spot it a mile off and you would come nowhere near meeting the Modern Studies Assignment's success criteria.

Passing off someone else's work as your own is called plagiarism. It is a big no–no for the Modern Studies Assignment and you should not even think about trying to do it for any work you ever do. Your teacher can tell what is your work and what is someone else's. The SQA can too. Taking notes and processing information from a range of sources are real skills which are not easy to do. Anyone can copy and paste.

In the Modern Studies Assignment at both National 4 and National 5 you need to use at least two sources, of different types. These different types can be primary and/or secondary sources.

Primary sources are those where you collect the information yourself. The kind of primary sources you are most likely to use are a survey of a group of people, an interview with a representative of an organisation or notes taken from a visiting speaker.

Secondary sources are information and/or data which have already been collected by somebody else. Websites, newspapers, magazines, blogs and books are all secondary sources.

SURVEY

A survey is an excellent way of gathering information. It makes your Modern Studies Assignment much more personal and unique. If you carry out your survey well, you can add real value to what you do. No matter what your topic or issue is, there are some things to take into consideration.

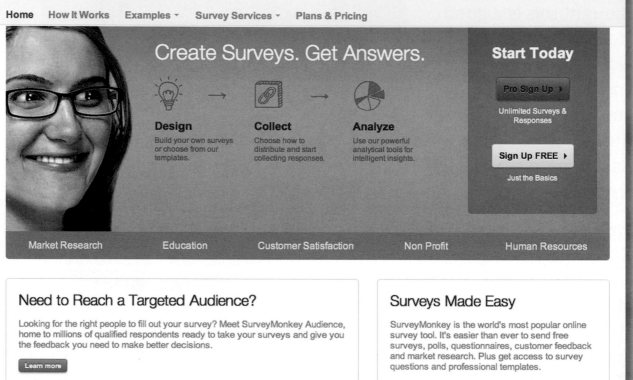

Size of sample: You should try to have at least 30 people respond to you. This will give your findings more validity.

Type of sample: Are you asking random people? If so why? Or, are you targeting people on the basis of their age, gender or experiences? If so why?

Questions. Are they closed or open or a bit of both? Closed questions are those where you restrict the responses, for example, YES/NO/DON'T KNOW. These responses are easier together and analyse. You can add up the number of 'YES' responses etc. Respondents often prefer to answer closed questions because they take far less time. You wish to start off with closed questions to 'warm up' your respondents then move on to open-ended questions. These are questions where the respondent is asked to explain what they think about a topic or issue. They allow the respondent to provide you with their true feelings and provide you with a much richer picture of the issue. It is though more difficult to compile conclusions to your survey as you may well have a more diverse set of responses than with the closed questions.

Try not to have 'leading' questions. This where your bias in framing the question leads your respondent towards a particular answer. For example, "How unfair do you think the First Past the Post voting system is?" is a leading question, whereas "Do you think First Past the Post is a fair voting system?" would be much more neutral.

You can plan your survey via an online provider such as SurveyMonkey (www.surveymonkey.com). A basic SurveyMonkey survey is completely free and enables you to design, select and organise/analyse your information in a professional way.

INTERVIEWS/NOTES FROM A VISITING SPEAKER

It may well be the case that you or a group of you carry out an interview with an expert in your chosen topic or issue. A visiting speaker to your school/college is also an excellent primary source of information and there are some basic ground rules you should remember. When contacting a person, always let him/her know what your focus is and the kind of information you are looking for. This will allow him/her to prepare for the interview/talk, perhaps bringing along extra information or pointing you to good sources. Have a pen/paper or even better, a Dictaphone to record the interview. Write up the answers as soon as you can while the interview is still fresh in your mind. Record the date, time and place of the interview. Taking a photograph is great, but remember to ask permission! Remember also to thank the expert/visiting speaker!

WEBSITES

Probably your first port of call should be the BBC website www.bbc.co.uk It is a fantastic resource for all things Modern Studies. It has a BBC Scotland version www.bbc.co.uk/scotland . The BBC news pages are wonderful and cover just about any topic or issue you could choose for your Assignment. So, you will find a lot to get you up and running on the BBC site.

Something else too. The BBC, by law, has to provide content which is impartial, that is, not biased towards any particular group or point of view. That's not to say that it's perfect.

The articles are written by human beings and even with the best of intentions there may be some bias or selection in the use of facts. But BBC journalists are trained to be as neutral as possible and you can trust the information you get from the BBC more than you would from a source which doesn't have to have these standards. Other news sites which you may find useful for Democracy in Scotland and the United Kingdom are STV (www.news.stv.tv), ITV (www.itv.com/news) and Channel 4 (www.channel4.com/news). These sites will also try and be impartial. They are not biased in favour of any particular group or cause.

Wikipedia (www.wikipedia.org) is also a good place to go when you first start out. It can give you a broad background to your topic or issue. Its main article can often give you new ideas or directions to follow. The main article will often have footnotes with references to other published articles which can be very handy too. But, be careful with Wikipedia. Wikipedia is a free, online encyclopaedia. Anyone can contribute to the articles. They are not written by professional journalists with the same standards as the BBC. Wikipedia is a wonderful resource and there are some great articles written and published for free by some really top people. But, the health warning is that some articles may or may not be completely accurate (some can even be deliberately inaccurate) and you should always check the accuracy of information you get on Wikipedia.

Most voluntary organisations, charities and pressure groups have professionally designed and maintained websites. Some are, of course, better than others in how they lay out their information as well as in the quality of the information they publish. Some are more upfront than others in stating what they believe in. For example, The Better Together pressure group (www.bettertogether.net) is against Scottish independence . It believes that the Scottish people are better off staying within the current devolved United Kingdom.

So, you should bear in mind what Better Together, or any other pressure group, believes in when reading its information. This is not to say that Better Together publishes inaccurate information. The information it publishes may well come from highly reputable sources such as university departments or respected political commentators. Likewise with Better Together's direct opposite, the pressure group Yes Scotland (www.yesscotland.net) Yes Scotland believes the opposite from Better Together. It believes that the Scottish people would be better off as an independent nation. Its 'evidence' may or may not be just as accurate or biased as Better Together's is. Your task is to read both views, and those of any others, and make your own mind up.

So, the key thing with information from all voluntary organisations, charities and pressure groups is not to accept their views and evidence uncritically. They may well be absolutely accurate. You may agree with all they stand for. That's fine, we all have views and we all support particular causes. Just show in your Modern Studies Assignment that that you are aware of potential issues of bias and that you have considered other points of view and other sources of evidence.

Another very good web–based place to find information is the websites of major opinion poll organisations. Ipsos–mori (www.ipsos–mori.com) has a wealth of opinion polls on a range of social issues. YouGov (www.yougov.co.uk) and Populous (www.populus.co.uk) are very good too. Just type your topic/issue into the search facility on the home page and there is a good chance you will find some published research which you can use as a source of information. Make sure that you take a careful note of when the research was carried out, the number of people interviewed and any key conclusions the opinion poll makes.

NEWSPAPERS

In the UK we have 'freedom of the press'. We treasure our freedom to offer our opinions and publish these in print or online for the public to read. This is not complete freedom of course. There are laws of libel which govern telling lies about individuals and groups. And there are laws which govern publishing offensive content about individuals and groups.

What it does mean is that, unlike the BBC, newspapers can be as biased and as one-sided as they like. Most newspapers support a political party and this viewpoint can colour the way the newspaper reports on events. Newspapers really should keep their views for their 'editorial' section, where they give their opinion on a particular issue or topic. Most newspapers still have such a feature. But many, especially the popular tabloids, extend their viewpoints into their reports. The popular tabloids often pick up on a theme such as benefit fraud or immigration and campaign on this on their front page or have regular 'special reports' where they publish their 'evidence'.

So, with newspapers, especially the tabloids, the same health warning exists as for pressure groups, charities and voluntary organisations. Consider potential issues of bias and don't accept what you read uncritically. Showing an awareness of the political background of a newspaper is always a good thing to do. Sales of printed newspapers are declining. Newspapers are having to adjust to the digital world and you will find the online versions of the newspapers to be of great help to your Modern Studies Assignment.

MAGAZINES

There are some magazines which have a special focus on UK social issues. You may find the language level in these magazines a bit tough but they are well worth having a go at if you come across them in your class or in the library.

Good ones are The Economist (www.economist.com), The New Statesman (www.newstatesman.com), The Week (www.theweek.co.uk). The same as with newspapers, magazines can support a particular viewpoint, so be aware of this too.

BLOGS

Part of the so-called 'new media', you are likely to come across blogs which are related to the topic or issue in your Modern Studies Assignment. Some blogs are very well written and informed. Some aren't! That's the beauty of modern communications. Anyone can set up a blog and publish what they think of an issue. It is good to refer to a good blog if you come across one, just remember again, that bloggers can have, as they say, 'an agenda' and can be biased towards a particular set of values. This is what motivates them to blog. Showing an awareness of what a blogger believes in as always a good thing to do.

BOOKS

Remember these? Books can go out of date in ways that websites don't. Maybe the date of the book's publication affects the content of what it is saying. It may be that what is written within a book, say in the 1980s now sounds very old-fashioned and has been overtaken by events. On the other hand, it may be that a very old book contains views and opinions that have stood the test of time. Books can be biased too. Being able to comment on the usefulness of a published book is very good practice in the Modern Studies assignment.

NATIONAL 4 MODERN STUDIES ASSESSMENT

Remember, in order to achieve the National 4 Modern Studies course award you must pass the internal assessments from the three units of the course:

- **Democracy in Scotland and the UK**

- **Social Issues in the United Kingdom**

- **International Issues**

- **The Added Value unit (the Modern Studies Assignment)**

Awards in National 4 Modern Studies are on a pass or fail basis.

Internal Assessment Democracy in Scotland and the UK

In order to pass this unit, you need to show evidence that you have achieved the national standard for National 4 Modern Studies.

Essentially you need to pass a skills assessment and a knowledge & understanding assessment. You may well sit both at the same time.

In the Democracy in Scotland and the UK unit, the skills you have to demonstrate are:

- **Detecting bias and/or exaggeration using two sources of information**

- **Briefly explaining bias and/or exaggeration using evidence from two sources of information**

In the Democracy in Scotland and the UK unit, you have to demonstrate knowledge & understanding of the kind of topics and issues contained in this textbook (although your teacher may well have taught you others which are equally appropriate). You have to:

- **Give straightforward descriptions of the main features of a political issue from either democracy in Scotland and/or the United Kingdom**

- **Give straightforward explanations relating to a political issue in Scotland and/or the United Kingdom**

There are a variety of ways in which you can show you have achieved the national standard. Your responses can be written, typed up, be in the form of a power point or other digital presentation or in the form of a poster.

THE ADDED VALUE UNIT (MODERN STUDIES ASSIGNMENT)

In order to pass the Added Value unit (The Modern Studies Assignment) you need to meet the national standard for National 4 Modern Studies.

In order to do this, you need to meet the success criteria (or 'assessment standards', to use the jargon).

1. CHOOSE AN APPROPRIATE MODERN STUDIES TOPIC OR ISSUE.

We have suggested several, but think for yourself too. What interests you in Modern Studies? Remember, you don't have to choose a social issue, you can choose a topic or issue from Scottish/British politics or International Issues. As well as what interests you now, think ahead to what you'd like to do after school. Is there a job/career you're interested in that Modern Studies is relevant to? Could your Assignment be handy for a course in further education you'd like to do? Could you learn things in your Assignment that would be good for a future job or impress a future employer?

Could your Assignment be handy for a course in further education you'd like to do? Could you learn things in your Assignment that would be good for a future job or impress a future employer?

2. COLLECT RELEVANT EVIDENCE FROM AT LEAST TWO SOURCES OF DIFFERENT TYPES.

These sources can be either

Primary sources such as surveys or interviews

or

Secondary sources such as websites, newspapers, magazines or textbooks

While you are thinking about your topic or issue, it's a good idea to think about how easy it will be to get the information you need. There's no point in doing a topic or issue where it will be very hard to gather information.

3. ORGANISE AND USE THE INFORMATION

One of the most relevant skills in Modern Studies is organising your information so that it makes sense to the reader. So, once you've gathered your information, organise it so that you discuss only the most relevant. Information can be irrelevant for lots of reasons; it could be out of date, it could be badly written, it could be full of jargon. On the other hand, valuable information is topical, provides reliable evidence and answers the key features of your topic or issue.

Always be on the look-out for information which is biased or selective in the use of facts. Always think; where does this information come from? Can I trust it? Might the person who wrote this or gathered the information be trying to make a point?

Using bar charts and/or pie charts is great and often explains issues better than words can. Always label your charts clearly always mentioning, if it was you who gathered the information, where and when you gathered it. Photographs are great too and the same good practice for charts applies here too.

4. DESCRIBE AND EXPLAIN SOME KEY FEATURES OF YOUR TOPIC OR ISSUE

This shows that you know and understand the main issues in your topic or issue. So, for example, if you choose to do a Modern Studies Assignment on a pressure group, such as Show Racism the Red Card (www.srtrc.org/resources/films/srtrc-scotland) you might want to describe the kind of activities SRTRC does to achieve its aims. For this topic, you will also have to explain issues, such as why racism continues to be an issue in Scotland and/or what progress has been made in tackling it.

All you are expected to show is that you are capable of looking at a political issue (or social or international if you choose an assignment topic from one of the other Modern Studies units) and explaining why it might have happened. If you can explain other points of view, so much the better as there is rarely in Modern Studies one single answer.

5. APPLY YOUR MODERN STUDIES SKILLS TO YOUR TOPIC OR ISSUE.

These can be either detecting bias and exaggeration or making decisions or drawing conclusions

You may come across a source that is completely biased or exaggerated and is therefore great to refer to in your Assignment.

Perhaps your issue or topic is one where Government has a decision to make about something. After referring to the evidence you have gathered, it will be very appropriate for you to state what you think should be done, giving reasons for your answer.

If you are drawing conclusions, don't just sum up what you have already written. Instead, comment on whether the issues you've researched have changed, got better, got worse, whether something has been successful or not or whether there are any trends over time.

Of course, it may just happen that you use all these skills and it would be foolish to leave a skill out just for the sake of it.

6. PRESENT YOUR FINDINGS.

This is where you have a lot of flexibility. What matters is that you can demonstrate your understanding of the topic or issue and that you have applied the Modern Studies skills. You have a variety of ways to present your findings.

You may choose to present your findings via a written report. Alternatively, you may choose to type up your report using Microsoft Word or some other software. A digital presentation via PowerPoint slides would also be acceptable. Your teacher will wish to retain a copy of your Assignment as it may be checked at some point by SQA.

However you choose to present your findings, use the following as a checklist:

- I have explained why I chose this topic or issue
- I have described and explained some of its key features
- I have collected information from at least two sources (name them, including the date you used them)
- I have organised and used these sources to describe and explain the key features of my topic or issue
- I have either commented on bias and exaggeration in sources

Or

- I have made a decision about my topic or issue

Or

- I have drawn conclusions about my topic or issue

NATIONAL 5 MODERN STUDIES ASSESSMENT

Remember, in order to achieve the National 5 Modern Studies course award you must pass the internal assessments from the three units of the course:

- **Democracy in Scotland and the UK**
- **Social Issues in the United Kingdom**
- **International Issues**

Then you have to pass the externally assessed (by SQA) Course Assessment.

The Course Assessment is composed of:

- **The National 5 Modern Studies Question Paper**
- **The National 5 Modern Studies Assignment**

The National 5 Modern Studies Course Assessment is out of 80 marks.

The National 5 Modern Studies Question Paper is worth 60 marks and lasts for one hour and 30 minutes. The Modern Studies National 5 Question Paper assesses knowledge, understanding and skills from the three units of the course.

The National 5 Modern Studies Assignment is out of 20 marks. In the National 5 Modern Studies Assignment you are required to research and gather information, having up to 1 hour to 'write up' your findings at your school/college under a high level of supervision and control.

Overall, after attempting both the internal and external assessments you can gain either an A, B, C or D in National 5 Modern Studies.

Internal Assessment Democracy in Scotland and the UK

In order to pass this unit, you need to show evidence that you have achieved the national standard for National 5 Modern Studies.

Essentially you need to pass a skills assessment and a knowledge & understanding assessment. You may well sit both at the same time.

In the Democracy in Scotland and the UK unit, the skills you have to demonstrate are:

- **Detecting exaggeration and/or selective use of facts**

using no less than two and no more than four sources of information

- **Explaining, in detail, exaggeration and/or selective use of facts using evidence from these sources of information**

In the Democracy in Scotland and the UK unit, you have to demonstrate knowledge & understanding of the kind of topics and issues contained in this textbook (although your teacher may well have taught you others which are equally appropriate). You have to:

- **Give detailed descriptions of a political issue from democracy in Scotland and/or the United Kingdom, providing factual and theoretical knowledge**

- **Give detailed explanations relating to a political issue in Scotland and/or the United Kingdom**

THE NATIONAL 5 MODERN STUDIES QUESTION PAPER (60 MARKS)

The National 5 Modern Studies Question Paper assesses both knowledge and understanding (34 marks) and Modern Studies skills (26 marks).

There are three sections to the Question Paper, based on the three units of the National 5 Modern Studies course.

Section 1 Democracy in Scotland and the UK unit   **(20 marks)**

Section 2 Social Issues in the United Kingdom unit   **(20 marks)**

Section 3 International Issues unit   **(20 marks)**

This textbook has been written in such a way as to prepare you for both the knowledge and understanding and the skills aspects of the National 5 Question Paper. While during your studies you will have concentrated mainly on either the Scottish or the UK context, you will also need to have a knowledge and understanding of the place of Scotland within the UK political system.

You can expect to see questions which require shorter, restricted responses worth from four marks up. You will also be given questions which require more extended and detailed description, explanation and analysis which can go up to ten marks. You will be tested on all the skills of the Modern Studies course; detecting and explaining exaggeration, selectivity in the use of facts, making and justifying a decision and drawing conclusions.

KNOWLEDGE AND UNDERSTANDING QUESTIONS

The number of marks allocated to a question indicates how much should be written. Marks in National 5 Modern Studies can go from 4–10. For 4 mark questions, two points will normally be expected. For six marks, three points will normally be expected. 10 mark questions will look for at least four points.

"Answers should contain relevant and up to date examples. Answers which are historical will not be credited as well as answers which are current."

Detail is the key at National 5. Your answers must answer the question which is set by the examiners, not the one you would like them to set! So, don't just write down all you know about an issue, answer the question the examiners have set for you.

The tried and tested Point, Explanation, Example isn't a bad way to approach these questions. So, if you were asked.

Question "Explain, in detail, why some people feel the Scottish Parliament should have more powers."

A good answer could look something like this...

Some people feel that the Scottish Parliament should have more powers because there are some areas in which the Scottish Parliament has no powers. For example, if the Scottish Parliament had power over immigration, Scotland could control how many people are allowed to come and live in Scotland.

Another reason is that Scottish voters have, for a long time now, had different political views than people in the south of England, where the Conservatives are still very popular. Some people in Scotland don't like the fact that a Conservative government can make decisions for Scotland when the Conservatives don't have much representation in Scotland.

Another reason, which is related to the above point, is that there are some inconsistencies with the arrangements we have at the moment. It isn't fair that an MP from Scotland can decide on education in England but an MP from England can have no say on education in Scotland. If Scotland had the full powers an independent country has, this problem wouldn't exist.

Lastly, some people would like the Scottish Parliament to have more powers because the ones Scotland does have worked well. Policies such as no tuition fees for Scottish students at Scottish universities have been popular and some people feel the Scottish people would be better off with a parliament with more powers.

SKILLS QUESTIONS

The skills which will be assessed in National 5 Modern Studies are

- **explaining exaggeration and selectivity in the use of facts**

- **giving detailed justifications for decisions**

- **giving detailed support for valid conclusions**

Note, the following are only illustrations of types of questions and should be seen as broad guidance on what each skill means. The SQA National 5 Specimen exam paper (and subsequent past papers) will provide you with the definitive picture of question stems and marking instructions)

EXPLAINING EXAGGERATION

In this type of question you are asked to explain why, using the source(s) a person is exaggerating in their statement. An exaggerated statement can say something is higher, lower, greater or smaller than it really is.

SOURCE 1 SCOTTISH TABLOID NEWSPAPERS, 2011– 2012

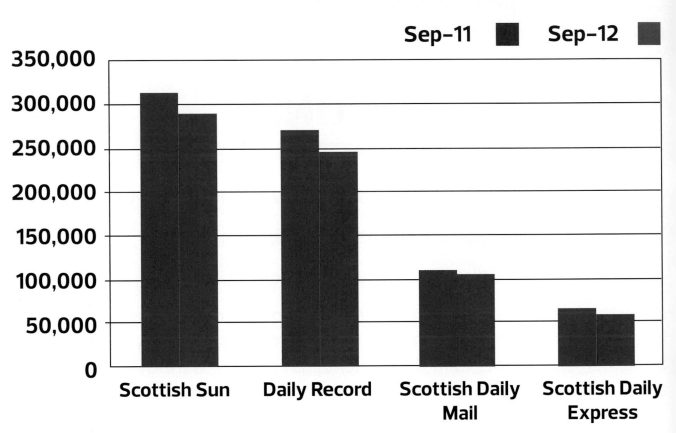

AVERAGE DAILY SALES

Sep–11 ■ Sep–12 ■

"Hardly anyone in Scotland buys a tabloid newspaper anymore." **Jim McGuire**

What evidence is there that Jim McGuire is exaggerating?

Jim McGuire is clearly exaggerating here. He claims that "hardly anyone in Scotland buys a tabloid newspaper anymore" and while sales for all the tabloids are down, many thousands of Scots still buy a tabloid newspaper every day.

EXPLAINING SELECTIVITY IN THE USE OF FACTS

In this type of question you are asked to explain why someone's viewpoint is being selective in the use of facts. On examining the sources you will find facts which do support particular statements within the point of view and others which do not. You may well be asked to come to an overall conclusion on the extent to which the person's viewpoint is selective in the use of facts.

So, you should show balance in your answer. There will be some evidence in the sources to support the viewpoint but there will be evidence in the sources that does not.

SOURCE 1: THE LEADERSHIP EFFECT IN THE 2011 SCOTTISH PARLIAMENT ELECTION

Opinion Polls showed SNP leader Alex Salmond to be the most popular candidate for First Minister. This resulted in the SNP putting Alex Salmond to the forefront of the party's campaign literature and broadcasts. The SNP also used "Scottish National Party (SNP) Alex Salmond for First Minister" on the second ballot paper.

A YouGov poll for the Scotland and Sunday newspaper showed voters across gender and social class to prefer Salmond to Scottish Labour leader Iain Gray to be Scottish First Minister. 56% of males preferred Salmond, with 30% choosing Gray. 48% of female voters preferred Salmond, with 25% choosing Gray. Even among working class voters who traditionally vote Labour, 53% chose Salmond with just 29% preferring Gray.

137

SOURCE 2: VOTER TURNOUTS AND PARTY PERFORMANCE, SELECTED CONSTITUENCIES, SCOTTISH PARLIAMENT ELECTION, 2011

Highest turnout	Party winner	Lowest turnout	Party winner
Eastwood 63.2%	SNP	Glasgow Provan 34.8%	LAB
Edinburgh Southern 61.6%	SNP	Glasgow Maryhill and Springburn 36.3%	LAB
Na h–Eileanan an Iar 59.6%	SNP	Glasgow Shettleston 37.9%	SNP
Edinburgh Western 59.4%	SNP	Glasgow Pollok 39.2%	LAB
Stirling 58.3%	SNP	Glasgow Kelvin 39.7%	SNP
East Lothian 57.1%	LAB	Glasgow Anniesland 43.2%	SNP
Edinburgh Pentlands 57.1%	SNP	Glasgow Southside 43.2%	SNP
Strathkelvin and Bearsden 56.9%	SNP	Cunninghame South 43.3%	SNP

VOTE

SOURCE 3: PARTY SUPPORT IN CONSTITUENCY AND REGIONAL VOTES, SCOTTISH PARLIAMENT ELECTIONS

Party	2003		2007		2011	
	Constituency	Region	Constituency	Region	Constituency	Region
SNP	23.8%	20.9%	32.9%	31.0%	45.4%	44.0%
LAB	34.6%	29.3%	32.1%	29.2%	31.7%	26.3%
CONS	16.6%	15.5%	16.6%	13.9%	13.9%	12.4%
LIBDEM	15.4%	11.8%	16.2%	11.3%	7.9%	5.2%
GREEN	0.0%	6.9%	0.1%	4.0%	0.0%	4.4%

SNP leader Alex Salmond is a politician who commands supports across all sections of the population. The SNP always gets its biggest support in the regional vote and when there is a low voter turnout. Labour lost most Scottish Parliament elections where there was a high turnout and continues to lose support in the constituency elections. **View of James Murray**

Explain in detail, the extent to which James Murray could be accused of being selective in the use of facts.

Use only Sources 1, 2 and 3.

In your answer you should

- **explain in detail why each of the statements made by James Murray are either correct or incorrect;**

- **reach an overall conclusion on the extent to which James Murray has been selective in the use of facts.**

So, a good answer could be.....

James Murray is correct when he says that SNP leader Alex Salmond is a politician who commands supports across all sections of the population. Source 1 tells us that more male, female and working class voters preferred him to Iain Gray as First Minister.

He is also correct when he says that "Labour lost most Scottish Parliament elections where there was a high turnout and continues to lose support in the constituency elections" as Source 2 tells us that Labour only won one constituency which had a high turnout and Source 3 tells us that Labour's percentage of the vote in constituency elections has gone down at every election since 2003.

However, he is incorrect when he says that "The SNP always gets its biggest support in the regional vote and when there is a low voter turnout." Source 3 shows that the SNP sometimes did better in the constituency vote Source 2 tells us that Labour, not the SNP, won the constituencies of Glasgow Provan and Maryhill where there were low turnouts.

James Murray is correct in two statements and incorrect in one, so he is only a little bit selective in his use of facts.

MAKING DECISIONS

Study Sources 1, 2 and 3 and the information about the two candidates, then answer the question which follows.

SELECTED FACTS ABOUT KILSHIRE

Kilshire is a local authority in central Scotland. It has a population of 287,000 which has been in decline in recent years due to its more affluent citizens moving into suburban local authorities.

SELECTED ECONOMIC STATISTICS

	Kilshire	Scotland	UK
Unemployed	25%	11.6%	10.6%
Average annual household income	£20,000	£25,000	£27,000
Children living in Poverty	35%	24%	20%
Average life expectancy	67 years	75 years	77 years

SOURCE 2: BRANDCO CASINO DEVELOPMENT

Brandco Plans

A large Asian company, Brandco, is seeking planning permission for a £120m casino and hotel complex. Included in the development are plans for affordable housing, a community sports facility and a health care centre. Brandco has predicted that 900 jobs will be created initially with possibly more to follow. Some of these will be highly paid but most will be at national minimum wage level.

The UK Government allows one regional or "super" casino, which can install Las Vegas–style machines with the potential for unlimited prizes. The casino and hotel complex would be built on currently disused land which has excellent links to major roads and both Glasgow and Edinburgh airports.

Say No to Brandco

A local pressure group has been set up to oppose the casino and hotel development. It has a number of concerns.

It is concerned at the debts which local people will run up. Studies have shown that those on low incomes are most vulnerable to gambling. The Las Vegas style–style machines will be cheap to play, offer big winnings but will have low pay–out returns.

It is also worried at the impact on the environment of the increased road traffic the development will generate. Noise and air pollution are problems which contribute to the poor overall health of Kilshire. It believes that the jobs will not be the skilled, well–paid ones Kilshire needs to improve its economy.

SOURCE 3: SURVEY OF PUBLIC OPINION IN KILSHIRE

	YES	NO	DON'T KNOW
Do you support the Brandco Casino development?	30%	60%	10%
Are you concerned about pollution in Kilshire?	60%	30%	10%
Are you concerned about poverty in Kilshire?	70%	20%	10%

SOURCE 4: INFORMATION ABOUT THE TWO CANDIDATES

Candidate A: Mike Spalding

In this election campaign I have been very enthusiastic about why the Brando development has to come to Kilshire.

Kilshire is a fantastic place to live and work. But let's not ignore the fact that average incomes here are around half the UK average. The Brandco development will create thousands of jobs right away. It may well lead to further investment as our community becomes more prosperous.

I accept that there are environmental issues to be addressed but more people in Kilshire are concerned about poverty than pollution. The planned development will be close to existing transport routes so fears over environmental pollution are misplaced. The reality is that families have bills to pay and mouths to feed. Child poverty in Kilshire is higher than any other part of Scotland. Let's work in partnership with Brandco to create a leisure destination which we can all be proud of.

Candidate B: Laura Gibson

Unlike Mike Spalding I'm here to represent the people of this community, not big business! Most people in Kilshire are against the Brandco development. I am against the proposal because it goes against all the UK Government's plans on casino developments.

I also worry about the effect gambling will have. Brandco's Las Vegas style gambling will push our low income families into deeper debt. We all know the links between poverty and bad health. Our life expectancy in Kilshire is below both the Scottish and the UK average. There are no plans to meet the wider health needs of our citizens.

I accept that unemployment in Kilshire is a serious concern. A quarter of our people are unemployed. But we need to maintain our quality of life. We need the right jobs, not jobs which will in the long-term make our social problems worse.

Use only the Information about the two Candidates and Sources 1, 2 and 3.

(i) State which candidate you think would be the more suitable to be selected as a Councillor for Kilshire.

(ii) Give three detailed reasons to support your choice.

(iii) Give two detailed reasons why you have rejected the other candidate.

In your answer, you must relate the "Information about the two Candidates" to the information in the Sources.

To get the best marks you need to refer to all the sources you are provided with. To write a good answer for this type of question, you should start off by stating clearly which option (or, in this case, which Candidate) you recommend. You can recommend either option, there is no option which is more correct than the other. You are marked according to how well you use the information to support your decision.

So, a good start could be to write

"There are two candidates; Mike Spalding and Laura Gibson who would both like to be elected as a Councillor in Kilshire. Kilshire is an area with a lot of unemployment and a large Asian company, Brandco, would like to open a new casino and hotel complex. Mike Spalding is in favour of Brandco's plans going ahead and Laura Gibson is against it. I have read all the sources of information about the candidates and the needs of Kilshire as a community. I have decided that the casino and hotel complex shouldn't go ahead and therefore support Laura Gibson.

In a new section, with a heading, you should give reasons for your decision. If you are able to 'synthesise' the sources, that is, link the together the written and statistical sources in your reasons, you will get better marks. For example;

Overall, I agree with Laura's main point that the casino and hotel complex would not be good for the people of Kilshire. Laura claims that "Most people in Kilshire are against the Brandco development". Source 3 shows that she is correct, 60% of residents are against Brandco.

A pressure group, "Say No to Brandco" (Source 2) is concerned at the debts local people will run up as people with low incomes are often tempted to gamble. Source 1 shows that a lot of people in Kilshire have low incomes. Average annual household income in Kilshire is way below the Scottish and UK average, something which Laura Gibson highlights in Source 4. Kilshire also has a higher percentage of people living in poverty than the rest of Scotland and the UK.

Lastly, Laura Gibson makes the point in Source 4 that "we need the right jobs, not jobs which will in the long-term make our social problems worse". Source 2 tells us that most of the jobs will be at national minimum wage level and even though 900 jobs will be created, there is no guarantee that there will be more jobs in the future.

You must then justify why you did not make the other choice. So, for example, you could write something like;

"I do not support Mike Spalding as while he is correct to say in Source 4 that "families have bills to pay and mouths to feed", he exaggerates the amount of jobs that will created by Brandco. He claims in Source 4 that "The Brandco development will create thousands of jobs right away". Source 2 states that only 900 jobs will be create to start with.

He also claims that average incomes in Kilshire are around half the UK average. Source 1 shows that he is exaggerating; average incomes are lower than in the rest of the country but they are not half of the UK average.

It is always good to add a final paragraph where you pull your arguments together.

"This was a difficult decision to make. Mike Spalding makes some good points and there is no doubt that Kilshire needs jobs and a financial boost. But, overall, I feel that Laura Gibson's views are the best. Gambling and debt would just make the lives of lower income people worse."

DRAWING CONCLUSIONS

In this type of question you are required to come to judgements based on the evidence. What you should not do is simply repeat what the sources tell you. Instead you are to interpret the sources and draw developed conclusions.

Developed conclusions are evidence based judgments on such as:

- **How successful a policy or initiative has been**

- **How effective a policy has been**

- **Whether statistics have changed significantly over time or whether they have stayed the same**

- **Comparisons between different groups**

Like the Making Decisions questions, if you can link and synthesise the sources in Drawing Conclusions questions, so much the better. Do not just re-write what is in the Source. You should try, if you can, to make an original and insightful conclusion of your own which is supported by more than one piece of valid evidence drawn from the Sources or from different parts of the same Source.

Study sources 1, 2, 3 and 4 below, then answer the question that follows.

SOURCE 1

The UK uses a range of voting systems for the different elections we have. Elections to the House of Commons use the First Past the Post (FPTP) voting system. Elections to the Scottish Parliament use the Additional Member System (AMS). UK Elections to the European Parliament (with the exception of Northern Ireland) use the Party list system. Elections to Scottish local authorities use the Single Transferable vote.

Each of the systems have their advantages and disadvantages. However, many people feel that we should have one system which is used for all elections and that it can be confusing having different systems for different elections. Many people are concerned at the low voter turnout for elections and there may be a connection between the type of system used and the number of people who vote. On the other hand, there may be other factors which account for low voter turnout, such as the issues within the constituency or the policies of the parties.

SOURCE 2: OPINION POLL
What is your preferred voting system?

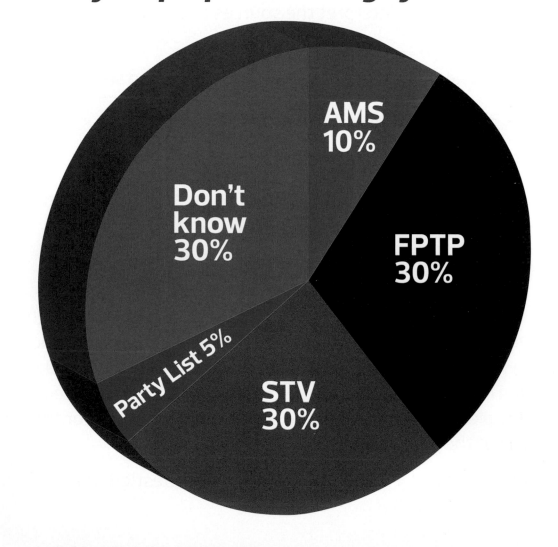

SOURCE 3: SHARE OF VOTE AND REPRESENTATION IN RECENT UK ELECTIONS

	2009 European Parliament (Party List)		2010 UK General Election (FPTP)		2011 Scottish Parliament (AMS)			2012 Scottish local council (STV)	
Party	% of vote	Seats won	% of vote	Seats won	% of vote (constituency)	% of vote (list)	Seats won	% of vote	Seats won
CON	27.7	26	36.1	306	12.4	13.9	15	13.2	115
Lab	15.7	13	29.0	258	26.3	31.7	37	31.3	394
Lib Dem	13.7	11	23.0	57	5.2	7.9	5	6.6	71
SNP	2.1	2	1.7	6	44.0	45.4	65	32.3	424

SOURCE 4: VOTER TURNOUT AT RECENT UK ELECTIONS

	2009 European Parliament (Party List)	2010 UK General Election (FPTP)	2011 Scottish Parliament (AMS)	2012 Scottish local council (STV)
Voter Turnout	34.5%	65.1%	50.4%	39.8%

Using sources 1, 2, 3 and 4, what conclusions can be drawn about voting systems in the UK?

You must reach a conclusion about at least one of the following:

- **public attitudes towards different voting systems**

- **party support and representation in different voting systems**

- **voter turnout in different voting systems**

You should compare information within and between the sources.

There are many conclusions which can be drawn from these Sources.

One example of a developed conclusion could be

"The FPTP voting system is unfair towards the Liberal Democrats but the public seem to quite like it".

Source 3 shows us that in the 2010 General election the Lib Dems won 23% of the vote but only 57 seats. This can be compared with Labour who won slightly more votes (29%) but far more seats (258). Despite this, Source 2 shows that FPTP is the most favourite voting system for the public.

Can you see how this is a developed conclusion? A statement is made which is original and insightful. It is then supported by evidence from more than one Source. Can you draw a different developed conclusion?

THE NATIONAL 5 MODERN STUDIES ASSIGNMENT (20 MARKS)

25% of your grade in National 5 Modern Studies comes from the Modern Studies Assignment. So this is your chance to 'bank' a good mark by doing the best work you possibly can. The bulk of the marks in the Modern Studies Assignment (14/20) come from your ability to demonstrate how you have acquired the skills of the course. The remaining 6 marks come from your knowledge and understanding of your chosen topic or issue. You are graded according to how well you meet the success criteria (or 'assessment standards', to use the jargon).

1. CHOOSE AN APPROPRIATE MODERN STUDIES TOPIC OR ISSUE.

We have suggested several, but think for yourself too. What interests you in Modern Studies? Remember, you don't have to choose a political issue, you can choose a topic or issue from Social Issues in the United Kingdom or International Issues. As well as what interests you now, think ahead to what you'd like to do after school. Is there a job/career you're interested in that Modern Studies is relevant to? Could your Assignment be handy for a course in further/higher education you'd like to do? Could you learn things in your Assignment that would be good for a future job or impress a future employer?

2. COLLECT RELEVANT EVIDENCE FROM AT LEAST TWO SOURCES OF DIFFERENT TYPES. THESE SOURCES CAN BE EITHER.

Primary sources such as surveys or interviews

or

Secondary sources such as websites, newspapers, magazines or textbooks

While you are thinking about your topic or issue, it's a good idea to think about how easy it will be to get the information you need. There's no point in doing a topic or issue where it will be very hard to gather information.

3. EVALUATE THE EFFECTIVENESS OF TWO RESEARCH METHODS, FOR EXAMPLE, THEIR STRENGTHS AND WEAKNESSES

One of the most relevant skills in Modern Studies is being able to evaluate the quality of your information.

You may have used a primary method of research such as a survey or an interview. How useful was it? Did it give you the answers you hoped for?

If so why? If not, why not? What about your secondary sources? What was good about the information you got from particular websites/newspapers/magazines/blogs? What wasn't so good?

Was the information which you received biased or selective in the use of facts? Were some sources more reliable and/or trustworthy than others?

4. APPLY YOUR MODERN STUDIES SKILLS TO YOUR TOPIC OR ISSUE.

If you are aware that a source of information is exaggerating or being selective in the use of facts, mention this in your Assignment. Perhaps your issue or topic is one where Government has a decision to make about a political issue. After referring to the evidence you have gathered, it will be very appropriate for you to state what you think should be done, giving reasons for your answer.

5. EXPLAIN AND ANALYSE SOME KEY FEATURES OF YOUR TOPIC OR ISSUE.

This shows that you know and understand the main issues in your topic or issue. So, for example, if you choose to do a Modern Studies Assignment on the impact of digital media campaigns on elections, you might want to describe what you mean by digital media campaigns. You also have to explain why digital media campaigns can have an impact and analyse whether digital media campaigns have made a significant difference to an election outcome. You are not expected to write a book on this or come up with the actual answer! There are people working away at universities trying to do this! All you are expected to show is that you are capable of looking at a political issue (or social or international if you choose an assignment topic from one of the other Modern Studies units) and explaining why it might have happened. If you can explain other points of view, so much the better as there is rarely in Modern Studies one single answer.

6. REACH A WELL-SUPPORTED CONCLUSION ABOUT YOUR TOPIC OR ISSUE WHICH IS SUPPORTED BY EVIDENCE.

Ultimately you should come to a conclusion about what you have learned. A good conclusion is NOT a re-statement of what you have already written. That is a summary, not a conclusion. A good conclusion can take many forms and will be different for different Assignments. But it should always be evidence based and could be a judgement around one of the following;

- **how successful or effective a course of action has been**

- **trends over time such as whether a problem is getting worse or whether improvements have been made**

- **how much different individuals or groups agree or disagree over solutions**

DEMOCRACY IN ACTION

Scotland's First Minister Alex Salmond and the UK Prime Minister David Cameron sign the historic Edinburgh Agreement which set in motion plans for a referendum on Scottish independence. Edinburgh, 15 October 2012.

Interested in knowing more?
Please visit **www.modernityscotland.co.uk**

DEMOCRACY IN SCOTLAND AND THE UNITED KINGDOM